Skills

This book is part of the Peter Lang Education list.
Every volume is peer reviewed and meets
the highest quality standards for content and production.

PETER LANG
New York • Bern • Berlin
Brussels • Vienna • Oxford • Warsaw

Mara Cogni

Skills

A Practical Guide in Conversation, Vocabulary and Writing

PETER LANG
New York • Bern • Berlin
Brussels • Vienna • Oxford • Warsaw

Library of Congress Cataloging-in-Publication Control Number: 2019023837

Bibliographic information published by **Die Deutsche Nationalbibliothek**.
Die Deutsche Nationalbibliothek lists this publication in the "Deutsche
Nationalbibliografie"; detailed bibliographic data are available
on the Internet at http://dnb.d-nb.de/.

ISBN 978-1-4331-5040-1 (paperback: alk. paper)
ISBN 978-1-4331-7130-7 (ebook pdf)
ISBN 978-1-4331-7131-4 (epub)
ISBN 978-1-4331-7132-1 (mobi)
DOI 10.3726/b15818

© 2019 Peter Lang Publishing, Inc., New York
29 Broadway, 18th floor, New York, NY 10006
www.peterlang.com

All rights reserved.
Reprint or reproduction, even partially, in all forms such as microfilm,
xerography, microfiche, microcard, and offset strictly prohibited.

CONTENTS

Introduction — vii

Chapter 1. Personal Skills
    Flexible — 3
    Diligent — 9
    Detail oriented — 13
    Proactive — 17
    Ambitious — 23
    Perseverant — 27
    Passionate — 31
    Empathetic — 35
    Self-sacrificing — 41
    Curious — 45
    Discipline — 49
    Sociable — 53
    Confident — 57
    Competitive — 61
    Courageous — 65

Chapter 2. General Skills
- Listening — 71
- Speaking — 77
- Reading — 83
- Writing — 89
- Communication — 95
- Cooperation — 101
- Observation — 107
- Responsibility — 113
- Problem solving — 119
- Conflict management — 125
- Critical thinking — 131
- Self-motivation — 137
- Digital competence — 143
- Emotional intelligence — 149
- Ethical reasoning — 155

Chapter 3. Skills and Jobs
- Healthcare — 163
- Mental healthcare — 169
- Childcare — 175
- Education — 181
- Engineering — 187
- Food service — 193
- Tradesmanship — 199
- Media and journalism — 205

Chapter 4. Skills for the Future
- Dealing with ambiguity — 213
- Avoiding confirmation bias — 219
- Cognitive flexibility — 225
- Deep focus — 231
- Dialectical thinking — 237

Chapter 5. Skills in Literature and Films — 243

References — 257

INTRODUCTION

Many students today have to grapple with the questions: *What am I very good at? What are my strengths and how can I use them for a better life?* These are central questions for us as learners, employees, family members, friends and thriving individuals. An inquiry into our skills helps us discover our potentialities and the talents we need to create a fulfilling life. As a result, it assists us in successfully finding the right role for ourselves in society. This book is intended to take learners on a reflective skill-investigative journey, in which speaking and writing about skills is both self-exploratory and fun.

Chapter 1 deals with *personal skills*, otherwise known as personal traits which make us different from others. They are our strengths in interpersonal relationships and in how we deal with life's various tasks. Chapter 2 deals with *general skills*, required in all fields of life, and which one can easily transfer from one field of work or life to another. Chapter 3 aims at connecting these skills with jobs, in which learners are also encouraged to do research into a third type of skills: *knowledge-based*. Chapter 4 introduces some *skills essential for the future*, and the final chapter places *skills into fictional contexts* which sheds a new light on the conversation about skills.

This book offers a more reflective approach to thinking and talking about skills. Learners will become well-equipped with knowledge and understanding of a set of skills they can ascribe to themselves and others. This will, consequently, prepare them for a world of work that is very specific in its skillset requirements. It also includes activities intended to expand vocabulary that is essential for successful communication. The book aims at helping students think critically about skills both orally and in writing.

CHAPTER 1

PERSONAL SKILLS

This chapter focuses on what we generally call personal skills, which refer to the things we are very good at and distinguish ourselves by. They represent our strengths and constitute our personality.

FLEXIBLE

1. SPEAKING

a. In groups, discuss the questions below. Take notes during your discussion.

1. Describe a flexible person.
2. Describe an uncompromising person.
3. What is workplace flexibility?
4. What is learning flexibility?
5. Are flexible people more competitive?
6. Is a flexible person confident or insecure?
7. Is flexibility the same as compromise?
8. Is being flexible the same as spontaneous?
9. What is the difference between cognitive and emotional flexibility?
10. Can anyone learn to become flexible?

> **Flexible** (adjective)
> ready to change in order to adapt to different circumstances
>
> **Flexibility** (noun)
> the willingness to change or find a middle ground

b. Use a dictionary to find antonyms for the words below.

- Rigid
- Categorical
- Unvarying
- Immovable

c. Discuss in groups.

1. What makes somebody unwilling to compromise? Make a list.
2. What makes somebody willing to compromise? Make a list.

2. WRITING

Write a short letter/e-mail to a person who is very rigid, in which you give advice about how she or he can become more flexible.

3. VOCABULARY

Underline one phrase which does not belong in each set.

1. A flexible employee / willing to compromise / willful attitude / open to shift strategy
2. Rigid rules / adaptable to change / changeable moods / malleable strategies
3. Easygoing environment / intransigent plans / cooperative efforts / adjustable colors

4. SPEAKING

a. Complete each statement with *one* of the alternatives provided (there is no right answer!). In groups, give reasons for your choice.

1. Flexible people _____
- change their minds a lot.
- are very accommodating.
- are not rigid.
- are open to change.

2. A flexible person _____
   - does not have unbending rules.
   - does not have any principles.
   - finds others smarter than himself/herself.
   - has little to say.

3. Adapting people _____
   - prefer to be liked.
   - prefer to conform than to rebel.
   - have a changeable temperament.
   - make the interlocutor feel special.

b. Discuss in groups. Explain your answers with reasons and examples.

1. Is it possible to be flexible and not like change?
2. Is having a changeable temperament an advantage?
3. Describe a person who makes their interlocutors feel special.
4. Is finding others more interesting than yourself, an advantage?
5. If you are very flexible, does it mean you have no established beliefs?

5. VOCABULARY

Complete the following words with their definitions below. Try to do this activity without a dictionary first. Compare your answer with a partner.

1. Adaptable _____
2. Unyielding _____
3. Malleable _____
4. Easygoing _____
5. Resilient _____
6. Inflexible _____
7. Stubborn _____
8. Single-minded _____
9. Persevering _____
10. Resolute _____

a. a person who is relaxed and tolerant
b. a person who does not adjust
c. a person concentrated on only one aim
d. a person who does not change attitude
e. a person who is uncompromising
f. a person who is easily influenced
g. a person who continues a course of action despite difficulties
h. a person who is purposeful and determined
i. a person who adjusts to new conditions
j. a person who recovers quickly

6. SPEAKING

a. Discuss in groups. Take notes during your discussion.

1. When is flexibility more important than persistence? Make a list of the benefits of being compromising rather than stubborn. Offer examples.
2. When is persistence more important than flexibility? Make a list of the benefits of being determined rather than compromising. Offer examples.
3. What is the difference between a stubborn child and a stubborn adult? Can stubbornness be positive?

b. Discuss in class. Take notes during your discussion.

WHAT IS BETTER: TOO MUCH COMPROMISE OR
NO COMPROMISE AT ALL?

- When is compromise more important than sticking to your own position?
- When is a no-compromise attitude the better choice?
- Which of the two options do you believe to be the best?

7. WRITING

Write a paragraph (about ten sentences) in which you discuss flexibility and persistence. Begin your paragraph with <u>one</u> of the topic sentences suggested below.

1. *Very often, flexibility is more important than determination.*
2. *Sometimes, determination is more important than flexibility.*

DILIGENT

8. SPEAKING

a. In groups, discuss the questions below. Use a dictionary and take notes during your discussion.

1. Describe a diligent person.
2. What is diligence in the workplace?
3. What is diligence at school?
4. How do diligent people view duty?
5. Is a diligent person more attentive or more focused?
6. Is it possible to be diligent but not committed?
7. Do diligent people like or dislike plans?
8. Are diligent people more meticulous or more ambitious?
9. Is diligence an attribute you can learn?
10. Is diligence a trait you can unlearn?

> **Diligent** (adjective)
> working carefully and constantly to accomplish something
>
> **Diligence** (noun)
> careful and persistent effort

b. Use a dictionary to find antonyms for the words below.

- NEGLIGENT
- IDLE
- UNORGANIZED
- IMPATIENT

c. Discuss in groups.

1. What makes somebody be very conscientious and follow rules diligently? Make a list.
2. What makes somebody act negligently and disinterested? Make a list.

9. WRITING

Write a short letter/e-mail to a person who is very negligent in their work. Give him/her advice on how they can become more diligent.

10. VOCABULARY

Underline one phrase which does not belong in each set.

1. A conscientious employee / willing to commit / casual attitude / open to strenuous effort
2. Hard-working students / tenacious learners / rigorous rules / lax attitudes
3. Dedicated workers / tireless dedication / idle activities / painstaking devotion

11. SPEAKING

a. Complete each statement with one of the alternatives provided (there is no right answer!). In groups, give reasons for your choice.

1. Diligent people _____
   - prioritize others more than themselves.
   - are reliable.
   - are persevering.
   - are driven.

2. A diligent person _____
   - is committed to long-term goals.
   - is not afraid of challenging work.
   - is single-minded.
   - is very studious.

3. Diligent people _____
   - are good at making plans.
   - keep themselves busy.
   - are predictable.
   - are rather tedious.

b. Discuss in groups. Explain your answers with reasons and examples.

1. What makes a person prioritize others rather than themselves?
2. Describe the personality of a person unafraid of challenging work.
3. Are predictable people more likeable than those who are unpredictable?
4. What makes somebody dull?
5. Is being fascinating more important than diligent?

12. VOCABULARY

Complete the following words with their definitions below. Try to do this activity without a dictionary first. Compare your answer with a partner.

1. Industrious _____
2. Conscientious _____
3. Meticulous _____
4. Persistent _____
5. Committed _____
6. Constant _____
7. Driven _____
8. Studious _____
9. Laid-back _____
10. Spontaneous _____

a. a person who wants to achieve success
b. a person who is unchangingly loyal and dependable
c. a person who spends a lot of time studying or reading
d. a person who is dedicated to something
e. a person who is relaxed in manner and character
f. a person who works hard
g. a person who does one's duty
h. a person who pays great attention to details
i. a person who often acts in an unplanned way
j. a person who keeps doing something even if it is hard

13. SPEAKING

a. Discuss in groups. Take notes during your discussion.

1. When is being diligent more important than laid-back? Make a list of the benefits of being diligent. Offer examples.
2. When is laziness more important than diligence? Make a list of situations when idleness is more important than diligence.
3. Does a child learn diligence differently from an adult?

b. Discuss in class.

WHAT IS BETTER: COMFORT OR ACHIEVEMENT?

- What makes a person seek comfort rather than achievement?
- What makes a person think achieving many things is more important than relaxation?
- Which option do you believe is the better one?

14. WRITING

Write a paragraph (about ten sentences) in which you discuss diligence and idleness. Begin your paragraph with <u>one</u> of the topic sentences suggested below.

1. *Very often, diligence is more important than idleness.*
2. *Sometimes, idleness is better than diligence.*

DETAIL ORIENTED

15. SPEAKING

a. In groups, discuss the questions below. Use a dictionary and take notes during your discussion.

1. Describe a detail oriented person.
2. Describe a detail oriented person at work.
3. Describe a detail oriented person at school.
4. Describe a detail oriented person at home.
5. Describe a detail oriented person with friends.
6. Do detail oriented people see the bigger picture?
7. Is a detail oriented person an interesting person?
8. Is it desirable for everyone to be detail oriented?
9. Can you be orderly without being thorough?
10. Can anyone learn to have an eye for detail?

> **Detail oriented** (adjective) paying attention to details and making sure something is done without errors

b. Use a dictionary to find antonyms for the words below.

- ABSENT-MINDED
- SCATTERED
- INDULGENT
- RECKLESS

c. Discuss in groups.

1. Why do some people believe that details are more important than the bigger picture? Make a list of their reasons.
2. Why do some people believe that the bigger picture is more important than the details? Make a list of their reasons.

16. WRITING

Write a short letter/e-mail to a person who is very inobservant in their work. Give them advice on how they can become more detail-attentive.

17. VOCABULARY

Underline one phrase which does not belong in each set.

1. a matter of no consequence / a thing of no importance / an unimportant point / a salient point
2. careless attitudes / particular employees / scrupulous considerations / accurate evaluations
3. a meticulous apprentice / a thorough examination / a particular interest / a technicality

18. SPEAKING

a. Complete each statement with one of the alternatives provided (there is no right answer!). In groups, give reasons for your choice.

1. Detail oriented people _____
- find it hard to let go.
- are strict with themselves and others.
- are free from error.
- are not bothered by distractions.

2. A detail oriented person _____
- is inquisitive.
- is afraid of consequences.
- is single-minded.
- is dull.

3. Detail oriented people _____
- are good at revising things.
- never get bored.
- are picky.
- are concerned with their reputation.

b. Discuss in groups. Explain your answers with reasons and examples.

1. Is being strict with yourself an advantage?
2. Is it possible to always avoid errors?
3. Is being picky a positive skill?
4. Is being concerned with your reputation an advantage?
5. Should we always revise our work?

19. VOCABULARY

Complete the following words with their definitions below. Try to do this activity without a dictionary first. Compare your answer with a partner.

1. Perfectionist _____
2. Attentive _____
3. Accurate _____
4. Scrupulous _____
5. Methodical _____
6. Fastidious _____
7. Fussy _____
8. Bookish _____
9. Pedant _____
10. Stickler for details _____

a. a person who is devoted to a lot of reading and studying
b. a person who is hard to please
c. a person who is very concerned about accuracy and details
d. a person who thinks that a particular type of behavior is very important
e. a person who demands the highest standard possible
f. a person who is very concerned with not making mistakes
g. a person who offers correct information and details
h. a person who pays close attention
i. a person who is systematic in thought and behavior
j. a person who is too interested in formal rules and details

20. SPEAKING

a. Discuss in groups. Take notes during your discussion.

1. When are details more important than the big picture? Make a list of the benefits of being detail oriented. Offer examples.
2. When is the whole more important than the details? Make a list of situations when seeing the bigger picture is more important than its details.
3. Why do some people pay more attention to details than others? How do we form this ability?

b. Discuss in class. Take notes during your discussion.

WHAT IS BETTER: TO BE TOO STRICT OR TOO INDULGENT WITH YOURSELF?

- What makes a person think that being strict with oneself and others is extremely important?
- What makes a person think that indulging is a better way of living one's life?
- Which option do you believe is the better one?

21. WRITING

Write a paragraph (about ten sentences) in which you discuss diligence and idleness. Begin your paragraph with <u>one</u> of the topic sentences suggested below.

1. *Very often, details are more important than the whole.*
2. *Sometimes, the bigger picture is more important than the details.*

PROACTIVE

22. SPEAKING

a. In groups, discuss the questions below. Use a dictionary and take notes during your discussion.

1. Describe a person who makes things happen.
2. Describe a person who waits for things to happen.
3. What does it take to change things?
4. Describe a proactive behavior in the workplace.
5. Describe a proactive behavior at school.
6. Describe a proactive social behavior.
7. Can a proactive person be afraid of confrontations?
8. Can a proactive person be afraid of standing out?
9. Can you be proactive and shy at the same time?
10. Can anyone learn to be proactive?

Proactive (adjective) taking action to make things happen rather than merely reacting to things when they happen

b. Use a dictionary to find antonyms for the words below.

- SHORTSIGHTED
- SLUGGISH
- NON-REACTIVE
- UNENTERPRISING

c. **Discuss in groups.**

1. Why do some people find it easy to take initiative and make things happen? Describe their personalities and attitudes.
2. Why do some people find it difficult to take initiative and change things? Describe their personalities and attitudes.

23. WRITING

Write a short letter/e-mail to a person who is listless and apathetic in their work. Give them advice on how they can become more proactive.

24. VOCABULARY

Underline one phrase which does not belong in each set.

1. take initiative / eager to act / enthusiastic engagement / reluctant participation
2. can-do attitudes / anxious reactions / dedicated employees / passionate learners
3. achieve results / high score / quiet observer / admirable accomplishments

25. SPEAKING

a. **Complete each statement with one of the alternatives provided (there is no right answer!). In groups, give reasons for your choice.**

1. Proactive people _____
   - do not see problems, only opportunities.
   - do not like others to decide for them.
   - are charismatic.
   - are concerned with how they are perceived by others.

2. A proactive person _____
- is impatient.
- is restless.
- is creative.
- is unpredictable.

3. Proactive people _____
- are good at making decisions.
- never get bored.
- are very ambitious.
- anticipate and prevent problems.

b. Discuss in groups. Explain your answers with reasons and examples.

1. Why do some people never get bored?
2. What skills help a person anticipate problems?
3. Can impatience be an advantage?
4. What makes a person charismatic?
5. Is being good at making decisions the same as making good decisions?

26. VOCABULARY

Complete the following words with their definitions below. Try to do this activity without a dictionary first. Compare your answer with a partner.

1. Go-getter _____
2. Passionate _____
3. Eager _____
4. Dynamic _____
5. Bursting _____
6. Extrovert _____
7. Patient _____
8. Unassertive _____
9. Meek _____
10. Charismatic _____

a. a person who is quiet and submissive
b. a person who is very lively and who has a lot of energy
c. a person who shows strong interests and enthusiasm
d. a person who can accept delays and problems
e. a person who inspires admiration in others
f. a person who is aggressively enterprising
g. a person who is very keen to make something happen
h. a person who is impatient because he/she wants to do so much
i. a person who is confident and happy in social situations
j. a person who does not show a confident personality

27. SPEAKING

a. Discuss in groups. Take notes during your discussion.

1. When is being proactive more important than being patient? Make a list of the benefits of taking initiative and making things happen. Offer examples.
2. When is patience more important than action? Make a list of situations when waiting instead of acting is preferred.
3. Are proactive people more successful than others?
4. How does one become proactive?

b. Discuss in groups.

WHAT IS BETTER: TO BELIEVE YOU CAN CONTROL EVERYTHING OR THAT YOU CAN CONTROL NOTHING?

- What are the advantages of believing that you can fix anything?
- What are the advantages of believing that you cannot really fix anything?
- Which option do you believe is the better one?

28. WRITING

Write a paragraph (about ten sentences) in which you discuss proactive and patient people. Begin your paragraph with <u>one</u> of the topic sentences suggested below.

1. *Very often, being proactive is the only way to make change happen.*
2. *Sometimes, patience is better than action.*

AMBITIOUS

29. SPEAKING

a. **In groups, discuss the questions below. Use a dictionary and take notes during your discussion.**

1. Describe an ambitious person.
2. What makes ambition different from goal?
3. Does everybody pursue success?
4. Give examples of career ambitions.
5. Give examples of educational ambitions.
6. Give examples of social ambitions.
7. Are ambitious people better at dealing with problems?
8. Do you need to be ambitious to improve your life?
9. Can you be ambitious and reserved at the same time?
10. Should everyone be ambitious?

Ambitious (adjective)
Having a strong wish to be successful, powerful, or rich

Ambition (noun)
A strong desire to achieve something

b. **Use a dictionary to find antonyms for the words below.**

- CONTENT
- HUMBLE
- FULFILLED
- SERENE

c. **Discuss in groups.**

1. Why are some people never content with how things are? Describe their personalities and attitudes.
2. Why are some people satisfied with just the way things are? Describe their personalities and attitudes.

30. WRITING

Write a short letter/e-mail to a person who is completely unenthusiastic in their work. Give them advice on how they can become more motivated.

31. VOCABULARY

Underline one phrase which does not belong in each set.

1. determined to succeed / go-ahead behavior / power-hungry attitude / anxious feelings
2. high aspirations / strong desires / feelings of contentment / lofty aims
3. ardent desire for fame / fierce ambition to succeed / complete satisfaction / desire to accomplish

32. SPEAKING

a. Complete each statement with one of the alternatives provided (there is no right answer!). In groups, give reasons for your choice.

1. Ambitious people _____
   - are power hungry.
   - never stop from self-improvement.
   - are perfectionists.
   - are concerned with how they are perceived by others.

2. An ambitious person _____
   - is outgoing.
   - is restless.
   - is insecure.
   - is unhappy.

3. Ambitious people _____
   - see life as a challenging puzzle that is never solved.
   - believe that hard work is everything life is about.
   - believe in the power of money.
   - want to leave the world a better place.

b. Discuss in groups.

1. Are power hungry people pleasant?
2. Should everybody strive to become better all the time?
3. Is being a perfectionist an advantage?
4. Is hard work a guarantee of success?
5. Is life a chore or a game?

33. VOCABULARY

Complete the following words with their definitions below. Try to do this activity without a dictionary first. Compare your answer with a partner.

1. Striving _____
2. Pushy _____
3. Aggressive _____
4. Avid _____
5. Demanding _____
6. Extravagant _____
7. Stiff _____
8. Formidable _____
9. Easy _____
10. Contented _____

a. a person who spends excessively
b. a person who is not friendly or relaxed
c. a person who is happy and satisfied
d. a person who is relaxed and free from worries
e. a person who shows a keen enthusiasm for something
f. a person who inspires fear or respect by being powerful
g. a person who behaves in a determined and forceful way
h. a person who makes great efforts to obtain something
i. a person who is unpleasantly self-confident
j. a person who makes others work hard and is not easily satisfied

34. SPEAKING

a. Discuss in groups. Take notes during your discussion.

1. What are the advantages of an ambitious way of life? Offer examples.
2. When is contentment more important than ambition? Make a list of situations when enjoying the way things are is better than striving for more.
3. Do ambitious people have better lives than others?
4. How does one become ambitious?

b. Discuss in class. Take notes during your discussion.

WHAT IS BETTER: TO BE EXTRAORDINARY OR TO BE ORDINARY?

- What are the benefits of being remarkable and admired by many?
- What are the benefits of being mediocre and unknown?
- Which option do you believe is the better one?

35. WRITING

Write a paragraph (about ten sentences) in which you discuss ambitious and contented people. Begin your paragraph with <u>one</u> of the topic sentences suggested below.

1. *Very often, being ambitious is the only way to make life better.*
2. *Sometimes, contentment is better than get-up-and-go.*

PERSEVERANT

36. SPEAKING

a. In groups, discuss the questions below. Use a dictionary and take notes during your discussion.

1. Describe a person who is insistent.
2. What makes somebody endure difficulties?
3. What makes somebody become tough?
4. When do we feel we want to give up?
5. Are there situations when we should give up?
6. Is being determined a weakness or a strength?
7. Is being exigent with yourself always beneficial?
8. Is being stubborn always a negative thing?
9. Is perseverance a guarantee of success?
10. Can anyone learn to be perseverant?

> **Perseverant** (adjective)
> continuing to do something even if it is difficult and demanding
>
> **Perseverance** (noun)
> persistence in doing something despite its difficulty

b. Use a dictionary to find antonyms for the words below.

- HESITANT
- APATHIC
- DISHEARTENED
- GLOOMY

c. Discuss in groups.

1. What makes people never give up when things get hard? Describe their personalities and attitudes.
2. What makes people give up when things become difficult? Describe their personalities and attitudes.

37. WRITING

Write a short letter/e-mail to a person who tends to give up plans and dreams when things get complicated. Give them advice on how they can become more perseverant.

38. VOCABULARY

Underline one phrase which does not belong in each set.

1. determined to succeed / commit to win / tireless attitude / feelings of indifference
2. steadfast rules / eager behaviors / undetermined directions / industrious learners
3. unstable emotions / firm belief / relentless dedication / unshakable dreams

39. SPEAKING

a. Complete each statement with one of the alternatives provided (there is no right answer!). In groups, give reasons for your choice.

1. Perseverant people _____
- believe that all dreams come true.
- hate to lose.
- are slaves to their own rules.
- are concerned with results.

2. A perseverant person _____
- is single-minded.
- is rigid.
- is obstinate.
- is unshakable.

3. Persevering people _____
- are irritatingly inflexible.
- believe that determination makes things happen.
- believe in the power of attitude.
- want to prove themselves better than others.

b. **Discuss in groups. Explain your answers with reasons and examples.**

1. Do our dreams always come true one way or another?
2. Is it beneficial to believe that all dreams come true?
3. What is the typical behavior of a person who is a slave of rules?
4. Is trying to prove you are better than others a virtue?
5. How can attitudes be powerful?

40. VOCABULARY

Complete the following words with their definitions below. Try to do this activity without a dictionary first. Compare your answer with a partner.

1. Persistent _____
2. Adamant _____
3. Tireless _____
4. Relentless _____
5. Enduring _____
6. Hardheaded _____
7. Tenacious _____
8. Pliable _____
9. Undecided _____
10. On the fence _____

a. a person who refuses to change his/her opinion or decision
b. a person who has not made a decision
c. a person who works hard without stopping
d. a person who avoids making a choice
e. a person who is unwilling to stop from trying to achieve something
f. a person who endures unfavorable situations
g. a person who makes decisions without the influence of emotions
h. a person who continues to do something even though it is difficult
i. a person who continues in a strict or harsh way
j. a person who is able to adapt to different situations

41. SPEAKING

a. Discuss in groups. Take notes during your discussion.

1. What are the advantages of perseverance? Offer examples.
2. When is renunciation more important than perseverance? Make a list of situations when giving up is better than persevering.
3. Do perseverant people have better lives than others?
4. How does one become perseverant?

b. Discuss in class. Take notes during your discussion.

WHAT IS BETTER: TO BELIEVE YOU ARE SUPERIOR TO OTHERS OR THAT OTHERS ARE SUPERIOR TO YOU?

- What are the attitudes and behaviors of people who believe they are better than others?
- What are the attitudes and behaviors of people who believe others are better than themselves?
- Which attitudes and behaviors do you favor?

42. WRITING

Write a paragraph (about ten sentences) in which you discuss perseverant and pliable people. Begin your paragraph with <u>one</u> of the topic sentences suggested below.

1. *Very often, perseverance is the only way to make your dreams come true.*
2. *Sometimes, renunciation is a better choice than perseverance.*

PASSIONATE

43. SPEAKING

a. In groups, discuss the questions below. Take notes during your discussion.

1. Describe an enthusiastic person.
2. Describe a dispassionate person.
3. Describe a fanatical person.
4. When do we say that a person is intense?
5. Do you like people who speak passionately?
6. Is being detached better than animated?
7. Is being passionate different from being impulsive?
8. Is passion different from desire?
9. Are passionate people inspiring?
10. Is it important to be passionate about things and people?

> **Passionate** (adjective) having or showing strong feelings or beliefs
>
> **Passion** (noun) a strong overwhelming emotion

b. Use a dictionary to find antonyms for the words below.

- UNENTHUSIASTIC
- NONCHALANT
- COLLECTED
- STANDOFFISH

c. Discuss in groups.

1. What makes some people be very passionate about things and people? Describe their personalities and attitudes.
2. What makes some people have a nonchalant relationship to things and people? Describe their personalities and attitudes.

44. WRITING

Write a short letter/e-mail to a person who lacks enthusiasm about their work and life. Give them advice on how they can become more passionate.

45. VOCABULARY

Underline one phrase which does not belong in each set.

1. Ungovernable emotions / animated conversations / wild ideas / half-hearted participations
2. Apathetic attitude / vigorous effort / fervent desire / animated spirit
3. Keen on achieving / hooked on getting results / disinterested in cracking it / crazy about victory

46. SPEAKING

a. Complete each statement with one of the alternatives provided (there is no right answer!). In groups, give reasons for your choice.

1. Passionate people _____
- have uncontrollable temperaments.
- are very energetic.
- are too eager.
- are melodramatic.

2. A passionate person _____
- is very romantic.
- is not a reasonable person.
- finds everything more interesting than himself/herself.
- is admirable.

3. Passionate people _____
- are devoted.
- are quick-tempered.
- are warm.
- are happier than the dispassionate.

PASSIONATE

b. Discuss in groups. Explain your answers with reasons and examples.

1. Are emotional people happier than others?
2. Can having an uncontrollable temperament be positive?
3. Are quick-tempered persons likeable?
4. What is the typical behavior of an overdramatic person?
5. Are emotions our friends or our foes?

47. VOCABULARY

Complete the following words with their definitions below. Try to do this activity without a dictionary first. Compare your answer with a partner.

1. Fiery _____
2. Keen on _____
3. Vehement _____
4. Energetic _____
5. Fanatical _____
6. Tumultuous _____
7. Eager _____
8. Wild _____
9. Emotional _____
10. Apathetic _____

a. a person who has a quick-tempered nature
b. a person who lacks discipline or control
c. a person who is excited and disorderly
d. a person who shows no interest or enthusiasm
e. a person who shows great activity and strength
f. a person who shows intense feelings
g. a person who is very interested on someone or something
h. a person who is obsessively concerned with something
i. a person who strongly wants to do or have something
j. a person who displays feelings openly

48. SPEAKING

a. Discuss in groups. Take notes during your discussion.

1. What are the advantages of being passionate? Offer examples.
2. When is coolness more important than passion? Make a list of situations when speaking or acting unemotionally is better than speaking or acting passionately.
3. Are passionate people more successful than others?
4. How does one become passionate?

b. Discuss in groups. Take notes during your discussion.

WHAT IS BETTER: A LIFE OF RESTLESS PASSION OR
A LIFE OF COMFORTABLE MONOTONY?

- Describe the life of a person who has many passions that take up all their time and energy.
- Describe the life of a person who has no passions or real interests.
- Which life do you prefer for yourself?

49. WRITING

Write a paragraph (about ten sentences) in which you discuss being passionate versus dispassionate. Begin your paragraph with <u>one</u> of the topic sentences suggested below.

1. *Very often, passion is the only way to make your dreams come true.*
2. *Sometimes, coolness is a better choice than passion.*

EMPATHETIC

50. SPEAKING

a. In groups, discuss the questions below. Take notes during your discussion.

1. Describe an empathetic person.
2. Describe an unconcerned person.
3. Describe an empathetic parent.
4. Describe an empathetic partner.
5. What are the jobs where empathy is crucial?
6. Can you be empathetic without being kind?
7. Can you be a good employee if you lack empathy skills?
8. Can you get along with others without showing empathy?
9. Is it possible to be understanding without being empathetic?
10. Is empathy a skill a person can learn?

Empathetic (adjective)
taking on another person's perspective and understand their feelings and emotions

Empathy (noun)
the ability to understand and share the feelings of another person

b. Use a dictionary to find antonyms for the words below.

- HARSH
- INSENSITIVE
- HOSTILE
- CALLOUS

c. Discuss in groups.

1. Why are some people able to take another person's perspective and try to feel what they feel? Describe their personalities and attitudes.
2. Why are some people unable to take another person's perspective and try to feel what they feel? Describe their personalities and attitudes.

51. WRITING

Write a short letter/e-mail to a person who lacks empathy in their work and life. Give them advice on how they can become more compassionate.

52. VOCABULARY

Underline one phrase which does not belong in each set.

1. walk in someone else's shoes / stay unaffected / feel somebody else's emotions / acknowledge somebody's needs
2. compassionate reactions / supporting actions / close contact / distressing disregard
3. emotional support / empathetic actions / detached evaluation / compassionate care

53. SPEAKING

a. Complete each statement with one of the alternatives provided (there is no right answer!). In groups, give reasons for your choice.

1. Empathetic people _____
   - understand more than they want to.
   - feel more than they want to.
   - are sensitive.
   - are sensible.

EMPATHETIC

2. An empathetic person _____
   - is very employable.
   - is bad at controlling emotions.
   - focuses too much on emotions.
   - is a good friend.

3. Empathetic people _____
   - are vulnerable to pain.
   - are less successful than others.
   - are more successful than others.
   - find others more important than themselves.

b. Discuss in groups. Explain your answers with reasons and examples.

1. Is being vulnerable to pain a positive thing?
2. Is a constant focus on emotions beneficial?
3. Is believing that other people are more important than ourselves advantageous?
4. Does understanding others make us like them?
5. Can a good friend lack empathy?

54. VOCABULARY

Complete the following words with their definitions below. Try to do this activity without a dictionary first. Compare your answer with a partner.

1. Compassionate _____
2. Friendly _____
3. Benevolent _____
4. Big-hearted _____
5. Sensitive _____
6. Supportive _____
7. Responsive _____
8. Understanding _____
9. Uninvolved _____
10. Impassive _____

a. a person who is very kind and generous
b. a person who is tolerant and forgiving of others' feelings and actions
c. a person who shows a quick appreciation of others' feelings
d. a person who is not concerned with somebody on an emotional level
e. a person who is kind and means well
f. a person who shows no feelings or emotions
g. a person who shows concern for others
h. a person who is kind and pleasant
i. a person who offers encouragement and emotional help
j. a person who reacts in a rapid and positive manner

55. SPEAKING

a. Discuss in groups. Take notes during your discussion.

1. What are the advantages of being empathetic? Offer examples.
2. When is emotional detachment more important than empathy? Make a list of situations when not sharing another person's feelings is better than feeling their emotions.
3. Are empathetic people more successful than others?
4. How does one become empathetic?

b. Discuss in class. Take notes during your discussion.

WHAT IS BETTER: TO UNDERSTAND OTHERS OR
TO LIKE THEM?

- Describe situations when it is easy to understand others, but difficult to like them.
- Describe situations when it is easy to like others, but difficult to understand them.
- Which alternative do you think is best?

56. WRITING

Write a paragraph (about ten sentences) in which you discuss being empathetic versus unemotional. Begin your paragraph with <u>one</u> of the topic sentences suggested below.

1. *Very often, empathetic people understand people and life better than others.*
2. *Sometimes, emotional detachment is a better choice than empathy.*

SELF-SACRIFICING

57. SPEAKING

a. In groups, discuss the questions below. Take notes during your discussion.

1. Describe a person who always prioritizes others rather than oneself.
2. Describe a person who is self-interested.
3. Describe a self-sacrificing parent.
4. Describe a self-sacrificing citizen.
5. Is being altruistic different from being kind?
6. Can one be self-sacrificing and intolerant at the same time?
7. When do we need to sacrifice our own interests?
8. When are we more important than others?
9. Is a relationship based on self-sacrifice a healthy one?
10. Should everyone be self-sacrificing?

Self-sacrificing (adjective) giving up one's own interest in order to help others or fight for a cause

Self-sacrifice (noun) renunciation to one's own wishes for the sake of others

b. Use a dictionary to find antonyms for the words below.

- GENEROUS
- DEVOTED
- INCONSIDERATE
- HEEDLESS

c. In groups, discuss the questions below.

1. What are the situations when self-sacrifice is necessary? Make a list.
2. What makes a person more self-sacrificing than others? Make a list.

58. WRITING

Write a short letter/e-mail to a person who tends to be self-centered. Give her/him suggestions about why they should take a back seat sometimes.

59. VOCABULARY

Underline one phrase which does not belong in each set.

1. reckless behavior / thoughtful comment / considerate question / selfless pursuit
2. kind words / thoughtless remark / cautious remark / sensitive person
3. tremendous dedication / deliberate renunciation / subtle suggestion / self-indulgent behavior

60. SPEAKING

a. Complete each statement with one of the alternatives provided (there is no right answer!). In groups, give reasons for your choice.

1. Self-sacrificing people _____
    - are tough-minded.
    - are not afraid of pain.
    - have low self-esteem.
    - live through others.

2. A self-sacrificing person _____
    - has no real beliefs.
    - is empathetic.
    - is compassionate.
    - is weak.

3. Self-sacrificing people _____
    - find themselves in the service of others.
    - find meaning in giving.
    - do not think they are important.
    - are concerned with public opinion.

b. Discuss in groups. Explain your answers with reasons and examples.

1. How do you define *meaning*? (Think about a meaningful relationship or a meaningful job.)
2. How do you define *happiness*?
3. Is meaning the same thing as happiness?
4. What makes compromise different from self-sacrifice?
5. Can self-sacrifice ever be self-serving?

61. VOCABULARY

Complete the following words with their definitions below. Try to do this activity without a dictionary first. Compare your answer with a partner.

1. Altruistic _____
2. Humanitarian _____
3. Tolerant _____
4. Forbearing _____
5. Accommodating _____
6. Merciful _____
7. Self-serving _____
8. Opportunistic _____
9. Insensitive _____
10. Ruthless _____

a. a person who shows no pity or compassion for others
b. a person who adjusts to somebody else's wishes
c. a person who uses situations in their favor
d. a person who shows no concern for people's feelings
e. a person who shows mercy
f. a person who shows concern for the well-being of others
g. a person who is concerned with promoting human welfare
h. a person who accepts opinions different from one's own
i. a person who is puts his own interests before those of others
j. a person who is patient and restrained

62. SPEAKING

a. Discuss in groups. Take notes during your discussion.

1. What are the advantages of being self-sacrificing? Offer examples.
2. What are the advantages of being self-serving? Make a list of situations when self-interest is useful.
3. Are self-sacrificing people as happy as others?
4. How does one become self-sacrificing?

b. Discuss in class. Take notes during your discussion.

ARE YOU HAPPIER BY BEING SELF-SACRIFICING OR SELF-SERVING?

1. When do people sacrifice their own wishes and interests for others?
2. When do people look out for themselves rather than others?
3. Does self-sacrifice increase or decrease personal happiness?

63. WRITING

Write a paragraph (about ten sentences) in which you discuss self-sacrifice versus self-interest. Begin your paragraph with <u>one</u> of the topic sentences suggested below.

1. *Self-sacrificing people find happiness in serving other people.*
2. *Sometimes, self-interest is the only way to find happiness.*

CURIOUS

64. SPEAKING

a. In groups, discuss the questions below. Take notes during your discussion.

1. Describe a curious person.
2. Describe an indifferent person.
3. Describe a curious child.
4. Describe a curious student.
5. Describe a curious worker.
6. Is learning without curiosity possible?
7. Can you improve yourself if you are incurious?
8. What is the opposite of curiosity?
9. Is being curious about somebody different from being curious about something?
10. Can anyone learn to be curious?

> **Curious** (adjective) interested in learning about people or things
>
> **Curiosity** (noun) a strong desire to know or learn something

b. Use a dictionary to find antonyms for the words below.

- UNCONCERNED
- JOYLESS
- DETACHED
- IMPASSIVE

c. Discuss in groups.

1. What makes people be curious and want to learn more about other people and things? Describe their personalities and attitudes.
2. What makes people be disinterested in other people and things? Describe their personalities and attitudes.

65. WRITING

Write a short letter/e-mail to a person who lacks curiosity in their work and life. Give them advice on how they can become more inquisitive and seeking.

66. VOCABULARY

Underline one phrase which does not belong in each set.

1. eager to learn / take an interest in / curious mind / indifferent behavior
2. an inquisitive audience / an absent interest / a curious investigator / a searching soul
3. a questioning motive / a total disinvolvement / an inquiring mind / a prying question

67. SPEAKING

a. Complete each statement with one of the alternatives provided (there is no right answer!). In groups, give reasons for your choice.

1. Curious people _____
- believe the world is a wonderful place.
- are more positive than incurious people.
- find learning enjoyable.
- are tolerant.

CURIOUS

2. A curious person _____
   - is very intelligent.
   - finds all people and things fascinating.
   - gets bored easily.
   - is not self-sufficient.

3. Curious people _____
   - are more educated.
   - are less insecure.
   - find others more interesting than themselves.
   - cannot control their impulses.

b. Discuss in groups. Explain your answers with reasons and examples.

1. Can one be smart and incurious?
2. Are all people fascinating?
3. How does a curious person deal with boredom?
4. Is there any relationship between education and curiosity?
5. Can one be intolerant and curious at the same time?

68. VOCABULARY

Complete the following words with their definitions below. Try to do this activity without a dictionary first. Compare your answer with a partner.

1. Nosy _____
2. Inquisitive _____
3. Intrusive _____
4. Analytical _____
5. Unique _____
6. Scrutinizing _____
7. Responsive _____
8. Mysterious _____
9. Commonplace _____
10. Bored _____

a. a person who responds with interest
b. a person who uses logical reasoning
c. a person who lacks interest in present activities
d. a person who shows too much interest in other people's affairs
e. a person who shows an interest in learning things
f. a person who is disruptive and annoying
g. a person who is remarkable and unusual
h. a person who examines closely and thoroughly
i. a person who is not interesting or original
j. a person who is difficult to explain

69. SPEAKING

a. Discuss in groups. Take notes during your discussion.

1. What are the advantages of being curious? Offer examples.
2. When is disinterestedness more important than curiosity? Make a list of situations when being incurious is better than being curious.
3. Are curious people more successful than others?
4. How does one become curious?

b. Discuss in class. Take notes during your discussion.

WHICH IS WORSE: NOSINESS OR APATHY?

- How does a nosy person behave?
- How does an apathetic person behave?
- Which of the two is the better choice?

70. WRITING

Write a paragraph (about ten sentences) in which you discuss being curious versus disinterested. Begin your paragraph with <u>one</u> of the topic sentences suggested below.

1. Very often, *curiosity is the only way to self-improvement.*
2. Sometimes, *a lack of interest is a better choice than curiosity.*

DISCIPLINE

71. SPEAKING

a. **In groups, discuss the questions below. Take notes during your discussion.**

1. Describe a disciplined person.
2. Describe an undisciplined person.
3. How do you know when a person likes order?
4. How do children learn discipline?
5. Can you be a good worker without being disciplined?
6. Is discipline based on order or duty?
7. Is discipline possible without rules?
8. Is discipline pleasant or unpleasant?
9. What motivates disciplined behavior?
10. Can anyone learn to be disciplined?

> **Disciplined** (adjective)
> showing a measured and controlled behavior or way of working
>
> **Discipline** (noun)
> A well-ordered behavior that obeys rules and follows a code of appropriate conduct

b. **Use a dictionary to find antonyms for the words below.**

- DISORDERLY
- UNRESTRAINED
- UNTRAINED
- INCONSISTENT

c. **Discuss in groups.**

1. What makes a person have a disciplined behavior? Describe their personalities and attitudes.

2. What makes some people be disorderly? Describe their personalities and attitudes.

72. WRITING

Write a short letter/e-mail to a person who lacks discipline in their work and life. Give them advice on how they can become more disciplined and organized.

73. VOCABULARY

Underline one phrase which does not belong in each set.

1. follow the rules / meet the requirements / fulfil one's duties / relaxing approach
2. have strong willpower / do sloppy work / show restraint / display orderly behavior
3. methodical work / ordered person / spontaneous questions / law-abiding citizens

74. SPEAKING

a. Complete each statement with one of the alternatives provided (there is no right answer!). In groups, give reasons for your choice.

1. Disciplined people _____
- follow rules religiously.
- are strict with others.
- are strict with themselves.
- are docile.

2. A disciplined person _____
- is very reliable.
- needs to have a schedule.
- likes control.
- is not spontaneous.

3. Disciplined people _____
- are good friends.
- are good employees.
- have rigid personalities.
- do everything easily.

b. Discuss in groups. Explain your answers with reasons and examples.

1. Why are some people more docile than others?
2. Is it an advantage to like control?
3. Can one be a disciplined employee and a disorderly parent?
4. Does a schedule make one more or less creative?
5. Is self-control more important than spontaneity?

75. VOCABULARY

Complete the following words with their definitions below. Try to do this activity without a dictionary first. Compare your answer with a partner.

1. Systematic _____
2. Obedient _____
3. Law-abiding _____
4. Orderly _____
5. Severe _____
6. Restrained _____
7. Discreet _____
8. Sloppy _____
9. Confrontational _____
10. Tidy _____

a. a person who deals with situations in an aggressive way
b. a person who is unemotional and dispassionate
c. a person who obeys the laws of society
d. a person who is careless and unsystematic
e. a person who acts according to a fixed plan or system
f. a person who keeps things in order

g. a person who fulfils an order or request
h. a person who is well behaved
i. a person who is stiff and unsmiling
j. a person who is careful in speech and actions

76. SPEAKING

a. Discuss in groups. Take notes during your discussion.

1. What are the advantages of being disciplined? Offer examples.
2. When is untidiness more important than discipline? Make a list of situations when being laidback is better than being orderly.
3. Are disciplined people more successful than others?
4. How does one become disciplined?

b. Discuss in class. Take notes during your discussion.

WHICH IS WORSE: AN UNDISCIPLINED OR AN UNHAPPY CHILD?

1. Describe the behavior of an undisciplined child.
2. Describe the behavior of an unhappy child.
3. Which is the worse alternative?

77. WRITING

Write a paragraph (about ten sentences) in which you discuss discipline versus indiscipline. Begin your paragraph with <u>one</u> of the topic sentences suggested below.

1. *Very often, disciplined people are successful at making their dreams come true.*
2. *Sometimes, indiscipline makes life less monotonous and predictable.*

SOCIABLE

78. SPEAKING

a. In groups, discuss the questions below. Take notes during your discussion.

1. Describe a sociable person.
2. Describe a shy person.
3. What makes people want to socialize?
4. What does an unsociable person like to do?
5. Are sociable people better friends?
6. Are all sociable people open-minded?
7. Is being sociable the same as kind?
8. Can you be sociable and lonely?
9. Can you be reserved and happy?
10. Can anyone learn to be sociable?

Sociable (adjective)
enjoying interacting with people and engaging in social activities

b. Use a dictionary to find antonyms for the words below.

- INSECURE
- PRIVATE
- INTROVERT
- ISOLATED

c. In groups, discuss the questions below.

1. What is a shy person afraid of? Make a list.
2. What is an anxious person afraid of? Make a list.

79. WRITING

Write a short letter/e-mail to a person who is very timid, in which you give advice about how she or he can become sociable.

80. VOCABULARY

Underline one phrase which does not belong in each set.

1. be friendly with strangers / enjoy other people's company / resent crowds / talk glibly
2. effortless conversation / eloquent speech / awkward silence / smooth talk
3. become embarrassed easily / mingle enthusiastically / respond quickly / navigate the conversation skillfully

81. SPEAKING

a. **Complete each statement with one of the alternatives provided (there is no right answer!). In groups, give reasons for your choice.**

1. Sociable people _____
   - are great listeners.
   - are great speakers.
   - are noisy.
   - are shallow.

2. A sociable person _____
   - is good at small talk.
   - gets tired easily.
   - is a fast thinker.
   - thrives in crowded places.

3. Social people _____
- are good friends.
- are good employees.
- have shifty personalities.
- are very likeable.

b. Discuss in groups. Explain your answers with reasons and examples.

1. Is it possible to be sociable and not like people?
2. Is having a shifty personality an advantage?
3. Are shallow people more enjoyable than those who are profound?
4. Is being a fast thinker the same as a fast learner?
5. What are the main skills of a good-natured person?

82. VOCABULARY

Complete the following words with their definitions below. Try to do this activity without a dictionary first. Compare your answer with a partner.

1. Alert _____
2. Outgoing _____
3. Demonstrative _____
4. Expressive _____
5. Eloquent _____
6. Hospitable _____
7. Liberal _____
8. Bigoted _____
9. Solitary _____
10. Extrovert _____

a. a person who is convincing in speaking and writing
b. a person who is intolerant of other people's beliefs
c. a person who lives alone and is isolated
d. a person who notices quickly unusual circumstances
e. a person who shows affection without restraint
f. a person who is socially confident

g. a person who welcomes visitors or guests
h. a person who communicates thoughts and feelings effectively
i. a person who loves meeting people
j. a person who is open to new ideas

83. SPEAKING

a. Discuss in groups. Take notes during your discussion.

1. What are the advantages of being sociable? Offer examples.
2. When is solitude more important than socialization? Make a list of situations when being unsociable is better than being sociable.
3. Are outgoing people more successful than others?
4. How does one become sociable?

b. Discuss in class. Take notes during your discussion.

WHAT IS BETTER: TO CARE TOO MUCH OR TO NOT CARE AT ALL?

1. When and why do people care a lot about what others think of them? Discuss their principles and values, as well as the consequences of being concerned with others' opinions.
2. When and why do people not care at all about what others think of them? Discuss their principles and values, as well as the consequences of such conduct.
3. Which is the better alternative?

84. WRITING

Write a paragraph (about ten sentences) in which you discuss being sociable versus being solitary. Begin your paragraph with <u>one</u> of the topic sentences suggested below.

1. *Very often, sociable people are happier and more successful than those who are unsociable.*
2. *Sometimes, solitude is a better choice than socialization.*

CONFIDENT

85. SPEAKING

a. In groups, discuss the questions below. Take notes during your discussion.

1. Describe a confident person.
2. Describe an uncertain person.
3. What is the typical behavior of a confident person?
4. Are confident people agreeable?
5. Is being confident the same as successful?
6. Can one be confident and vulnerable?
7. Can one be confident and anxious?
8. Is being confident the same as brave?
9. Is *seeming* confident the same as *being* confident?
10. Can anyone learn to be confident?

> **Confident** (adjective)
> feeling and showing certainty in one's aptitudes and qualities
>
> **Confidence** (noun)
> A feeling of conviction in one's own abilities and qualities

b. Use a dictionary to find antonyms for the words below.

- HUMBLE
- FEARFUL
- UNASSERTIVE
- UNPRETENTIOUS

c. In groups, discuss the questions below.

1. What makes a person feel insecure? Make a list.
2. What makes people believe in themselves? Make a list.

86. WRITING

Write a short letter/e-mail to a person who is very insecure, in which you give advice about how she or he can become more confident.

87. VOCABULARY

Underline one phrase which does not belong in each set.

1. confident in her abilities / self-assured attitudes / fearless behavior / humble request
2. courageous proposal / bold move / diffident manner / certain deal
3. is secure in her belief / has no doubts / is cool-headed in meetings / shows pessimistic outlooks

88. SPEAKING

a. Complete each statement with one of the alternatives provided (there is no right answer!). In groups, give reasons for your choice.

1. Confident people _____
   - are very likeable.
   - are great speakers.
   - are inspiring.
   - are arrogant.

2. A confident person _____
   - cares about appearances.
   - is a good communicator.
   - does not care about others' opinions.
   - is a great leader.

3. Confident people _____
   - are arrogant.
   - are more successful.
   - believe they are better than others.
   - believe in the power of attitudes.

c. Discuss in groups. Explain your answers with reasons and examples.

1. Is it possible to fake confidence?
2. Is it possible to fake humility?
3. Are confident people focused on others or themselves?
4. Is confidence inspiring?
5. Is self-doubt instructional?

89. VOCABULARY

Complete the following words with their definitions below. Try to do this activity without a dictionary first. Compare your answer with a partner.

1. Sanguine _____
2. Cheerful _____
3. Radiant _____
4. Unworried _____
5. Collected _____
6. Poised _____
7. Cool-headed _____
8. Jumpy _____
9. Fretful _____
10. Steady _____

a. a person who is not anxious or nervous
b. a person who is not easily worried or provoked
c. a person who is clearly happy and optimistic
d. a person who is reliable and self-restrained
e. a person who is calm and self-controlled
f. a person who is positive in difficult situations
g. a person who emanates joy and health
h. a person who has an elegant behavior
i. a person who feels and expresses frustration and discomfort
j. a person who get easily anxious or tense

90. SPEAKING

a. Discuss in groups. Take notes during your discussion.

1. What are the advantages of being confident? Offer examples.
2. What are the advantages of being in doubt? Make a list of situations when being unsure is advantageous.
3. Are confident people more successful than others?
4. How does one become confident?

b. Discuss in class. Take notes during your discussion.

WHICH IS BETTER: CERTAINTY OR DOUBT?

1. How do people who are confident speak and act? Make a list of the reasons why people are convinced that their beliefs and opinions are absolute.
2. How do people who are insecure speak and act? Make a list of the reasons why people have doubts about their beliefs and opinions.
3. Which is the better alternative?

91. WRITING

Write a paragraph (about ten sentences) in which you discuss certainty versus uncertainty. Begin your paragraph with <u>one</u> of the topic sentences suggested below.

1. *Very often, confident people are more successful than those who are insecure.*
2. *Sometimes, doubt is more beneficial than confidence.*

COMPETITIVE

92. SPEAKING

a. **In groups, discuss the questions below. Take notes during your discussion.**

1. Describe a competitive person.
2. Describe a noncompetitive person.
3. What is the typical behavior of a competitive person?
4. Are competing people agreeable?
5. Is being competitive different from being ambitious?
6. Can one be competitive and cooperative?
7. When is competition constructive?
8. When is competition destructive?
9. Can you be successful if you do not desire success?
10. Is being competitive a desirable skill?

> **Competitive** (adjective)
> Having and showing a strong desire to be more successful than others
>
> **Competition** (noun)
> an activity to win and establish one's superiority over others

b. **Use a dictionary to find antonyms for the words below.**

- COOPERATIVE
- HARMONIOUS
- NONCONFLICTING
- MUTUAL

c. **In groups, discuss the questions below.**

1. What makes a person wish to be more successful than others? Make a list.
2. What makes people cooperate with others and share their gains? Make a list.

93. WRITING

Write a short letter/e-mail to a person who lacks a sense of competitiveness, in which you give advice about how she or he can become more competitive.

94. VOCABULARY

Underline one phrase which does not belong in each set.

1. ambitious dreams / high aspirations / humble desires / combatant behavior
2. antagonistic attitude / dog-eat-dog approach / militant manner / mutual understanding
3. rival teams / ambitious tendencies / collaborative work / opposing outlooks

95. SPEAKING

a. Complete each statement with one of the alternatives provided (there is no right answer!). In groups, give reasons for your choice.

1. Competitive people _____
 - are unfriendly.
 - are great businessmen.
 - are respected.
 - are feared.

2. A competitive person _____
 - is disrespectful.
 - is attracted to power.
 - has high self-esteem.
 - is brave.

3. Competitive people _____
 - are afraid of failure.
 - make progress happen.
 - are uncompromising.
 - are not afraid of failure.

COMPETITIVE 63

b. **Discuss in groups. Explain your answers with reasons and examples.**

1. Can real friends be competitive with each other?
2. Is it wrong to be attracted to power?
3. Can you become better at your job without competing with others?
4. Is progress without competition possible?
5. What would a world with no competition look like?

96. VOCABULARY

Complete the following words with their definitions below. Try to do this activity without a dictionary first. Compare your answer with a partner.

1. Adversary _____
2. Challenger _____
3. Pushy _____
4. Domineering _____
5. Bullying _____
6. Enterprising _____
7. Adventurous _____
8. Bold _____
9. Emulous _____
10. In league _____

a. a person who communicates his/her wishes in an arrogant manner
b. a person who is confident and courageous
c. a person who conspires with others
d. a person who intimidates vulnerable people
e. a person who is unpleasantly confident
f. a person who shows initiative and creativity
g. a person who is an opponent in a contest
h. a person who engages in a contest
i. a person who takes risks and tries out new experiences
j. a person who seeks to imitate someone or something

97. SPEAKING

a. Discuss in groups. Take notes during your discussion.

1. What are the advantages of being competitive? Offer examples.
2. What are the advantages of being cooperative? Make a list of situations when cooperating is gainful.
3. Are competitive people happy?
4. How does one become competitive?

b. Discuss in class. Take notes during your discussion.

WHAT IS BETTER: TO BE LOVED OR TO BE RESPECTED?

1. When do people love us?
2. When do people respect us?
3. Which is the better alternative?

98. WRITING

Write a paragraph (about ten sentences) in which you discuss being competitive versus being cooperative. Begin your paragraph with <u>one</u> of the topic sentences suggested below.

1. *Very often, competitive people are more successful than those who are non-competitive.*
2. *Sometimes, cooperation is a better choice than competition.*

COURAGEOUS

99. SPEAKING

a. **In groups, discuss the questions below. Take notes during your discussion.**

1. Describe a courageous person.
2. Describe a cowardly person.
3. What is the typical behavior of a courageous person?
4. Are courageous people always confident?
5. Is being courageous different from being strong?
6. Can one be brave and shy at the same time?
7. When do we need courage?
8. Why do we need courage?
9. Can you change things if you lack courage?
10. Can anyone learn to be brave?

> **Courageous** (adjective) showing no fear of danger or pain
>
> **Courage** (noun) brave behavior in face of pain or grief

b. **Use a dictionary to find antonyms for the words below.**

- AFRAID
- SHY
- COWARDLY
- FEARFUL

c. **In groups, discuss the questions below.**

1. What are the situations when courage is fundamental? Make a list.
2. What makes a person show more courage than others? Make a list.

100. WRITING

Write a short letter/e-mail to a person who lacks courage, in which you give advice about how she or he can become more courageous.

101. VOCABULARY

Underline one phrase which does not belong in each set.

1. brave activists / heroic behaviors / fearless actions / fearful voices
2. bold move / adventurous spirit / cautious remark / confident manner
3. timid comment / determined approach / audacious suggestion / daring escape

102. SPEAKING

a. Complete each statement with one of the alternatives provided (there is no right answer!). In groups, give reasons for your choice.

1. Courageous people _____
   - are reckless.
   - are great partners.
   - are highly respected.
   - are fighters.

2. A courageous person _____
   - is not afraid to fail.
   - is not afraid of pain.
   - accepts loss easily.
   - is a problem-solver.

3. Courageous people _____
   - are naive.
   - make progress happen.
   - overthink everything.
   - like to act rather than think.

b. Discuss in groups. Explain your answers with reasons and examples.

1. What makes people have fears?
2. How do we behave when we are afraid?
3. Does fear have any purpose?
4. Is change without courage possible?
5. Can you be brave and still be afraid?

103. VOCABULARY

Complete the following words with their definitions below. Try to do this activity without a dictionary first. Compare your answer with a partner.

1. Adventurous _____
2. Tough _____
3. Fearless _____
4. Dynamic _____
5. Spirited _____
6. Unflinching _____
7. Unalarmed _____
8. Irresolute _____
9. Weak _____
10. Cowardly _____

a. a person who has positive attitudes and is full of energy
b. a person who shows no fear
c. a person who shows a lack of courage
d. a person who is not anxious or nervous
e. a person who endures difficulty and pain
f. a person who is hesitant or uncertain
g. a person who is enthusiastic and determined
h. a person who takes risks and tries out new experiences
i. a person who shows no hesitation in the face of danger
j. a person who does not stand up for her beliefs

104. SPEAKING

a. Discuss in groups. Take notes during your discussion.

1. What are the advantages of being courageous? Offer examples.
2. What are the advantages of being cautious? Make a list of situations when caution is useful.
3. Are courageous people better-off than others?
4. How does one become brave?

b. Discuss in class. Take notes during your discussion.

WHEN IS FACING DANGER A BETTER CHOICE THAN STAYING SAFE?

1. When do people take risks?
2. Make a list of dangerous situations.
3. Is taking risks more admirable than staying safe?

105. WRITING

Write a paragraph (about ten sentences) in which you discuss taking risks versus staying safe. Begin your paragraph with <u>one</u> of the topic sentences suggested below.

1. *Courageous people create their own destiny and thus are admirable people.*
2. *Sometimes, caution is a better choice than risk.*

CHAPTER 2

GENERAL SKILLS

> *This chapter focuses on what we generally call transferable or functional skills. They are the skills that can be transferred across various fields of activity, which makes them universal. They are the skills present in all aspects of our lives, and which bear significance for our good functioning in the workplace and society in general.*

LISTENING

1. SPEAKING

a. In groups, discuss the questions below. Take notes during your discussion.

1. What are listening skills?
2. What is the difference between listening and hearing?
3. What are the elements of active listening?
4. How is listening to a song different from listening to a radio program?
5. How do you listen to something you know nothing about in advance?
6. How do you listen to something when you want to get specific details to discuss later?
7. How does listening help you communicate?
8. How do you listen to understand a speaker's feelings?
9. How do you listen to understand a speaker's reasoning?
10. How do you transform passive listening into an active process?

b. Rank the five alternatives according to their importance. In groups, give reasons for your ranking.

An excellent listener

- ☐ maintains eye contact.
- ☐ shows understanding.
- ☐ asks follow-up questions.
- ☐ never interrupts.
- ☐ keeps an open mind.

c. **Answer the following questions with Yes or No. Explain your answers to a partner or in groups.**

AM I A GOOD LISTENER IF:

- ☐ I listen only to what is being said and not what is left unsaid?
- ☐ I notice contradictions between verbal and non-verbal communication?
- ☐ I prefer to think people mean what they say?
- ☐ I interrupt my interlocutor if I have questions?
- ☐ I listen with the purpose of reacting to what is being said?
- ☐ I put the speakers at ease and encourage them to share their thoughts?
- ☐ I get bored and distracted if the speaker communicates things I find uninteresting?
- ☐ I get impatient if speakers take long pauses in their speeches?
- ☐ I separate a person's irritating habits from the contents of their speech?
- ☐ I fail to integrate the speaker's volume and tone in the overall message?

d. **Consult a dictionary to answer the questions below.**

1. What are the typical attitudes of good listeners? Make a list of adjectives to describe them.
2. What are the typical behaviors of good listeners? Make a list of verbs to describe them.

2. WRITING

a. **Write a paragraph in which you explain and give examples of different ways to improve listening skills. Begin your paragraph with the topic sentence suggested below.**

There are many ways we can use to improve listening skills.

b. **Write a paragraph in which you discuss the importance of listening skills in different domains of life. Begin your paragraph with the topic sentence suggested below.**

Clearly, listening skills are important in all spheres of life.

3. SPEAKING

Complete each statement with one of the alternatives provided. In groups, give reasons for your choice.

1. Good listeners _____
   - are able to stay focused for long periods of time.
   - believe people always mean what they say.
   - believe people rarely mean what they say.
   - focus on the whole message and ignore details.

2. Effective listeners _____
   - pay close attention to what is being spoken.
   - think about what to ask next.
   - find others more interesting than themselves.
   - have little to say.

3. Successful listeners _____
   - need time before they can respond.
   - do not need to ensure they understood the message.
   - show interest and curiosity.
   - pay attention to relevant details for later use.

4. GRAMMAR AND WRITING

Change the following verbs into adjectives. Use them to describe people in complete sentences. Follow the example.

1. OBSERVE—OBSERVANT
   An observant person notices and pays attention to his/her surroundings.

2. MIND
   _____

3. CARE
   _____

4. DISCERN
   _____

5. CONSIDER
   _____

5. SPEAKING

Discuss in groups. Take notes during your discussion.

1. What makes us pay attention?
2. What makes us ignore something or somebody?
3. What makes listening a demanding activity?
4. What is a good listener concerned with?
5. When is listening more important than speaking?
6. Is responding more important than understanding when we listen?
7. Is remembering more important than evaluating when we listen?
8. When do we listen for enjoyment?
9. Is listening for enjoyment different from listening to learn?
10. Is attention more important than empathy in active listening?

6. ESSAY WRITING

This activity is for everyone who wants to practice thinking and writing clearly. You can use all previous notes and write an essay in which you discuss listening skills. You can follow the guiding instructions provided below. Remember to give your essay a title.

	LISTENING SKILLS
ONE	Write an introduction in which you point out the importance of listening skills.
TWO	Write a paragraph in which you discuss the significance of *listening skills at school*. In addition, show how we can develop them. Give examples of situations in which these skills offer huge benefits.
THREE	Write a paragraph in which you discuss the importance of *listening skills at work*. In addition, indicate how we can improve them. Give examples of situations in which these skills offer numerous gains.
FOUR	Write a paragraph in which you discuss why some people might find it hard to be active listeners. Give examples and explanations of how and why *listening skills should be practiced* deliberately and systematically in order to make them part of your skill set.
FIVE	Write a conclusion in which you discuss how important listening is in all spheres of life.

SPEAKING

7. SPEAKING

  a. In groups, discuss the questions below. Take notes during your discussion.

  1. What are speaking skills?
  2. Describe a person who speaks eagerly.
  3. Describe a person who speaks convincingly.
  4. Describe a person who speaks half-heartedly.
  5. Do we always communicate when we speak?
  6. How is speaking to a group of friends different from speaking to a group of colleagues?
  7. Does speaking include or exclude listening?
  8. Can you be a great speaker without a broad vocabulary?
  9. Can you be an effective speaker without practice?
  10. How can we develop speaking skills?

  b. Rank the five alternatives according to their importance. In groups, give reasons for your ranking.

An excellent speaker

- ☐ pronounces words clearly.
- ☐ rephrases ideas when the audience seems to struggle to understand them.
- ☐ always prepares in advance.
- ☐ presents thoughts and ideas in a structured and logical manner.
- ☐ uses humor and tells stories to engage the audience.

c. **Answer the following questions with Yes or No. Explain your answers to a partner or in groups.**

AM I AN EFFECTIVE SPEAKER IF:

- ☐ I rarely get my message across?
- ☐ I struggle with engaging with my audience?
- ☐ I encourage people to participate and ask questions?
- ☐ I pay attention to my body language and tone of voice?
- ☐ I am not afraid of pausing to gather my thoughts?
- ☐ I always use notes when I speak in public?
- ☐ I memorize what I am going to say and never change my memorized message?
- ☐ I tell a joke if I forget what I should say next?
- ☐ I avoid repeating words and ideas?
- ☐ I am not afraid of failing or making mistakes?

d. **Consult a dictionary to answer the questions below.**

1. What are the typical attitudes of effective speakers? Make a list of adjectives to describe them.
2. What are the typical behaviors of effective speakers? Make a list of verbs to describe them.

8. WRITING

a. **Write a paragraph in which you explain and give examples of different ways to improve speaking skills. Begin your paragraph with the topic sentence suggested below.**

There are many ways we can use to improve speaking skills.

b. **Write a paragraph in which you discuss the importance of speaking skills in different domains of life. Begin your paragraph with the topic sentence suggested below.**

Clearly, speaking skills are important in all spheres of life.

9. SPEAKING

Complete each statement with one of the alternatives provided. In groups, give reasons for your choice.

1. Good speakers _____
- make every word count.
- are confident in the messages they communicate.
- are exceptionally observant.
- are remarkably articulate.

2. Effective speakers _____
- ignore their audience and focus on their message.
- enunciate clearly and speak loudly.
- plan everything in advance.
- do not pause excessively.

3. Successful speakers _____
- control their emotions.
- use a lot of humor.
- avoid monotonous presentations.
- offer relevant examples to their audiences.

10. GRAMMAR AND WRITING

Change the following nouns into adjectives. Use them to describe people in complete sentences. Follow the example.

1. HUMOR—HUMOROUS
A humorous person is funny and makes people laugh.

2. CLARITY
_____

3. ARTICULATION
_____

4. PREPARATION
   _____

5. TENSION
   _____

11. SPEAKING

Discuss in groups. Take notes during your discussion.

1. What makes us want to speak?
2. When do we need to speak?
3. What makes speaking a challenging activity?
4. Is speaking confidently more important than speaking clearly?
5. Is information more important than flexibility when we speak?
6. Is communication more significant than understanding when we speak?
7. What is effective speaking in a job interview?
8. What is effective speaking on an exam?
9. Is attention of greater import than empathy when we speak?
10. Is a skillful speaker more calculated or more spontaneous?

12. ESSAY WRITING

This activity is for everyone who wants to practice thinking and writing clearly. You can use all previous notes and write an essay in which you discuss *speaking skills*. You can follow the guiding instructions provided below. Remember to give your essay a title.

	SPEAKING SKILLS
ONE	Write an introduction in which you point out the importance of speaking skills.
TWO	Write a paragraph in which you discuss the significance of *speaking skills at school*. In addition, show how we can develop them. Give examples of situations in which these skills offer huge benefits.
THREE	Write a paragraph in which you discuss the importance of *speaking skills at work*. In addition, indicate how we can improve them. Give examples of situations in which these skills offer numerous gains.
FOUR	Write a paragraph in which you discuss why some people might find it hard to be effective speakers. Give examples and explanations why *speaking skills should be practiced* deliberately and systematically in order to make them part of your skill set.
FIVE	Write a conclusion in which you discuss how important speaking is in all spheres of life.

READING

13. SPEAKING

a. In groups, discuss the questions below. Take notes during your discussion.

1. What are reading skills?
2. What are reading strategies?
3. Describe an avid reader.
4. How is reading an article different from reading a novel?
5. How does reading fiction help us develop empathy skills?
6. How does reading expand our understanding?
7. What makes *reading to enjoy* different from *reading to learn*?
8. What makes reading a book different from watching a film?
9. What is the relation between reading and thinking?
10. How can we develop reading skills?

b. Rank the five alternatives according to their importance. In groups, give reasons for your ranking.

An excellent reader

- ☐ reads daily.
- ☐ reads different types of texts.
- ☐ rereads and asks questions about the text.
- ☐ challenges herself with difficult texts.
- ☐ reads intensively to build vocabulary.

c. **Answer the following questions with Yes or No. Explain your answers to a partner or in groups.**

AM I A COMPETENT READER IF:

- ☐ I maintain concentration when I read long texts?
- ☐ I easily identify the main points and arguments in a text?
- ☐ I give up when I read texts with advanced language?
- ☐ I am aware of the purpose of my reading?
- ☐ I never read what I deem difficult?
- ☐ I do not think it is important to pause and reflect when I read?
- ☐ I fail to identify key words and ideas?
- ☐ I always try to rephrase and summarize the main ideas of a text?
- ☐ I read fast and forget to take notes while reading?
- ☐ I frequently guess the meaning of words from their context?

d. **Use a dictionary to answer the questions below.**

1. What are the typical attitudes of skilled readers? Make a list of adjectives to describe them.
2. What are the typical behaviors of skilled readers? Make a list of verbs to describe them.

14. WRITING

a. **Write a paragraph in which you explain and give examples of different ways to improve reading skills. Begin your paragraph with the topic sentence suggested below.**

There are many ways we can use to improve reading skills.

b. **Write a paragraph in which you discuss the importance of reading skills in different domains of life. Begin your paragraph with the topic sentence suggested below.**

Clearly, reading skills are important in all spheres of life.

15. SPEAKING

Complete each statement with one of the alternatives provided. In groups, give reasons for your choice.

1. Avid readers _____
- like to learn about different lives.
- have extensive vocabulary.
- are very smart.
- have great empathy skills.

2. A skilled reader _____
- is disciplined.
- has great concentration skills.
- is curious.
- has a rich imagination.

3. Enthusiastic readers_____
- are interested in the world around them.
- are lifelong learners.
- like to escape reality.
- find reading an adventurous experience.

16. GRAMMAR AND WRITING

Change the following adjectives into nouns. Use them to describe people in complete sentences. Follow the example.

1. IMAGINATIVE—IMAGINATION
   A person who reads a lot develops a rich imagination.

2. FOCUSED
   _____

3. CONNECTED
   _____

4. CHALLENGING
   _____

5. INSPIRING
   _____

17. SPEAKING

Discuss in groups. Take notes during your discussion.

1. What makes us want to read?
2. How has technology changed the way we read?
3. What are the benefits of reading?
4. What makes reading different from writing?
5. How does reading improve writing?
6. Can you be an efficient learner without being a systematic reader?
7. What differentiates an avid reader from a dispassionate one?
8. Describe a disinterested reader.
9. What advice would you give to a dispassionate reader?
10. What is the relation between reading and thinking?

18. ESSAY WRITING

This activity is for everyone who wants to practice thinking and writing clearly. You can use all previous notes and write an essay in which you discuss reading skills. You can follow the guiding instructions provided below. Remember to give your essay a title.

	READING SKILLS
ONE	Write an introduction in which you point out the importance of reading skills.
TWO	Write a paragraph in which you discuss the significance of *reading skills at school*. In addition, show how we can develop them. Give examples of situations in which these skills offer huge benefits.
THREE	Write a paragraph in which you discuss the importance of *reading skills at work*. In addition, indicate how we can improve them. Give examples of situations in which these skills offer numerous gains.
FOUR	Write a paragraph in which you discuss why some people might find it hard to be effective readers. Give examples and explanations why *reading skills should be practiced* deliberately and systematically in order to make them part of your skill set.
FIVE	Write a conclusion in which you discuss how significant reading is in all spheres of life.

WRITING

19. SPEAKING

a. In groups, discuss the questions below. Take notes during your discussion.

1. What are writing skills?
2. Describe an eminent writer.
3. How does writing help us organize our thoughts?
4. What makes written communication different from verbal communication?
5. What are typical writing tasks at school?
6. What are typical writing tasks at work?
7. What makes writing clear and coherent?
8. What makes academic writing different from a blog post?
9. What differentiates an application letter from a diary?
10. Can you be a skilled writer without practice?

b. Rank the five alternatives according to their importance. In groups, give reasons for your ranking.

An excellent writer

- ☐ reads books and expands his vocabulary.
- ☐ tries to be the reader of her own text.
- ☐ offers appropriate examples and uses varied vocabulary.
- ☐ gives reasonable explanations for her opinions.
- ☐ uses clear and consistent language.

c. Answer the following questions with Yes or No. Explain your answers to a partner or in groups.

AM I A COMPETENT WRITER IF:

☐ I do a lot of research before I write an academic text?
☐ I make sure each paragraph I write focuses on one main idea?
☐ I make references to reliable sources in my texts?
☐ I focus on the size of the text and get easily repetitive?
☐ I easily mix up verbs, nouns, adjectives and adverbs?
☐ I do not think it is important to plan my text before I write it?
☐ I read every writing task carefully and underline key words to focus on?
☐ I believe it is essential to give reasons to the claims I make in my texts?
☐ I like to write speedily and finish as fast as possible?
☐ I sometimes use words whose meanings I do not entirely know?

d. Consult a dictionary to answer the questions below.

1. What are the typical attitudes of eminent writers? Make a list of adjectives to describe them.
2. What are the typical behaviors of eminent writers? Make a list of verbs to describe them.

20. WRITING

a. Write a paragraph in which you explain and give examples of different ways to improve writing skills. Begin your paragraph with the topic sentence suggested below.

There are many ways we can use to improve writing skills.

b. Write a paragraph in which you discuss the importance of writing skills in different domains of life. Begin your paragraph with the topic sentence suggested below.

Clearly, writing skills are central in all spheres of life.

WRITING

21. SPEAKING

Complete each statement with one of the alternatives provided. In groups, give reasons for your choice.

1. Competent writers _____
   - plan their texts carefully.
   - use varied vocabulary.
   - are very creative.
   - have great communication skills.

2. A skilled writer _____
   - writes regularly.
   - uses complex sentences.
   - thinks and communicates clearly.
   - has a lot to say.

3. Eminent writers _____
   - are eminent readers.
   - check their texts for spelling and grammar mistakes.
   - reread their texts before submitting them.
   - are exceptionally logical.

22. GRAMMAR AND WRITING

Change the following adjectives into adverbs. Use them to describe people in complete sentences. Follow the example.

1. CAREFUL—CAREFULLY
   A good writer chooses words and ideas carefully.

2. SYSTEMATIC
   _____

3. ORDERED
   _____

4. CONSISTENT
   _____

5. COHERENT
   _____

23. SPEAKING

Discuss in groups. Take notes during your discussion.

1. What makes us want to write?
2. How has technology changed the way we write?
3. How does reading improve writing?
4. Has the blogosphere made writing better or worse?
5. What makes a writer popular?
6. Describe the language of an emotional writer.
7. Describe the language of a rational writer.
8. What is the relation between writing and thinking?
9. Is writing regular posts on Facebook a form of writing practice?
10. Is content more consequential than language in written communication?

24. ESSAY WRITING

This activity is for everyone who wants to practice thinking and writing clearly. You can use all previous notes and write an essay in which you discuss writing skills. You can follow the guiding instructions provided below.

	WRITING SKILLS
ONE	Write an introduction in which you point out the importance of writing skills.
TWO	Write a paragraph in which you discuss the significance of *writing skills at school*. In addition, show how we can develop them. Give examples of situations in which these skills offer huge benefits.
THREE	Write a paragraph in which you discuss the importance of *writing skills at work*. In addition, indicate how we can improve them. Give examples of situations in which these skills offer numerous gains.
FOUR	Write a paragraph in which you discuss why some people might find it hard to be effective writers. Give examples and explanations why *writing skills should be practiced* deliberately and systematically to make them part of your skill set.
FIVE	Write a conclusion in which you discuss how significant writing is in all spheres of life.

COMMUNICATION

25. SPEAKING

a. In groups, discuss the questions below. Take notes during your discussion.

1. What are communication skills?
2. What are the most common means of communication?
3. Describe a good communicator (both in terms of writing and speaking skills).
4. Describe a poor communicator (both in terms of writing and speaking skills).
5. Which type of communication is more spontaneous?
6. Is a good communicator an active listener or an active speaker?
7. Is clarity more important than empathy in communication?
8. Is honesty more important than respect in communication?
9. How can one become good at written communication?
10. How can one become good at verbal communication?

b. Rank the five alternatives according to their importance. In groups, give reasons for your ranking.

An excellent communicator

- ☐ is patient and open-minded.
- ☐ communicates clearly and encouragingly.
- ☐ expresses beliefs in a convincing manner.
- ☐ shows empathy and consideration.
- ☐ speaks straightforwardly.

c. **Answer the following questions with Yes or No. Explain your answers to a partner or in groups.**

AM I AN EFFECTIVE COMMUNICATOR IF:

- ☐ I often find it challenging to get my messages across?
- ☐ I am assertive and express my beliefs in a direct manner?
- ☐ I seem persuasive both in written and verbal form?
- ☐ I need time to think before I respond?
- ☐ I listen with the purpose of reacting to what is being said?
- ☐ I am spontaneous and respond to what happens in the moment?
- ☐ I have a deep understanding of myself and others?
- ☐ I am nervous and tend to forget my ideas when I speak in public?
- ☐ I read people's body language and adjust the content of my speech?
- ☐ I focus on details and often forget my train of thought?

d. **Consult a dictionary to answer the questions below.**

1. What are typical attitudes of good communicators? Make a list of adjectives to describe them.
2. What are typical behaviors of good communicators? Make a list of verbs to describe them.

26. WRITING

a. **Write a paragraph in which you discuss some ways to improve communication skills. Begin your paragraph with the topic sentence suggested below.**

Communication skills can be improved in numerous ways.

b. **Write a paragraph in which you discuss the importance of communication skills in different domains of life. Begin your paragraph with the topic sentence suggested below.**

Clearly, communication skills are important in all spheres of life.

COMMUNICATION

27. SPEAKING

Complete each statement with one of the alternatives provided. In groups, give reasons for your choice.

1. An effective communicator _____
   - is attentive to details.
   - is an active listener.
   - is good with words.
   - is a clear thinker.

2. A successful communicator _____
   - makes eye contact.
   - pays attention to others' body language.
   - uses a lot of body language.
   - is friendly.

3. A good communicator_____
   - is honest.
   - is confident.
   - is empathetic.
   - is open-minded.

28. GRAMMAR AND WRITING

Change the following adverbs into verbs. Use them to describe people in complete sentences. Follow the example.

1. SIMPLY—simplify
   A person who simplifies complex messages can communicate them effectively.

2. EXPRESSIVELY
   _____

3. DIRECTLY
   _____

4. SPECIFICALLY
   _____

5. RESPECTFULLY
   _____

29. SPEAKING

Discuss in groups. Take notes during your discussion.

1. What makes us want to communicate something?
2. When do we choose to write rather than speak?
3. When do we choose to speak rather than write?
4. Is verbal communication more effective than written communication?
5. Is online communication better than offline communication?
6. Can you become good at communicating without practice?
7. Is effective communication a skill anyone can learn?
8. Can you be convincing without being a good communicator?
9. Can you communicate clearly without thinking clearly?
10. Why is communication an important skill in life?

30. ESSAY WRITING

This activity is for everyone who wants to practice thinking and writing clearly. You can use all previous notes and write an essay in which you discuss communication skills. You can follow the guiding steps provided below.

	COMMUNICATION SKILLS
ONE	Write an introduction in which you point out the importance of communication skills at school, at work, with friends, and life in general.
TWO	Write a paragraph in which you discuss the significance of *communication skills at school*. In addition, show how we can develop them. Give examples of situations in which communication skills offer huge benefits.
THREE	Write a paragraph in which you discuss the importance of *communication skills at work*. In addition, indicate how we can improve them. Give examples of situations in which these skills offer numerous gains.
FOUR	Write a paragraph in which you discuss the significance of *communication skills at social events*. In addition, specify how we can cultivate them. Give examples of situations in which these skills offer many advantages.
FIVE	Write a conclusion in which you discuss how important communication is in all spheres of life.

COOPERATION

31. SPEAKING

a. In groups, discuss the questions below. Take notes during your discussion.

1. What makes us want to cooperate with others?
2. When do we need to cooperate with others?
3. Describe a person who is bad at collaborating with others.
4. Describe a person who is good at teaming up.
5. When is cooperation a crucial skill?
6. Is it possible to never work together with others?
7. Give examples of collaboration at school.
8. Give examples of collaboration in the workplace.
9. How can we become good team players?
10. How is cooperation related to knowledge?

b. Rank the five alternatives according to their importance. In groups, give reasons for your ranking.

An excellent team player

- ☐ is open to help and offer feedback.
- ☐ socializes outside work/school.
- ☐ is not afraid to learn from criticism.
- ☐ tries to reduce differences and conflicts.
- ☐ is optimistic.

c. **Answer the following questions with Yes or No. Explain your answers to a partner or in groups.**

AM I A GOOD TEAM PLAYER IF:

☐ I accept feedback and comments on my work with an open mind?
☐ I am reluctant to share my ideas with others?
☐ I am unsure about the validity of my beliefs and values?
☐ I am good at settling disputes?
☐ I tend to get impatient when I have to wait indeterminately for others?
☐ I tend to speak more than listen?
☐ I trust my own ideas more than others'?
☐ I demonstrate concern for other people's viewpoints?
☐ I am competitive and eager to get my point across?
☐ I make decisions based on the majority's choices?

d. **Use a dictionary to answer the questions below.**

1. What are the typical attitudes of good team players? Make a list of adjectives to describe them.
2. What are the typical behaviors of good team players? Make a list of verbs to describe them.

32. WRITING

a. **Write a paragraph in which you discuss some ways to improve cooperation skills. Begin your paragraph with the topic sentence suggested below.**

There are diverse ways you can use to improve your cooperation skills.

b. **Write a paragraph in which you discuss the importance of collaboration skills in different domains of life. Begin your paragraph with the topic sentence suggested below.**

Clearly, cooperation skills are important in all spheres of life.

33. SPEAKING

Complete each statement with one of the alternatives provided. In groups, give reasons for your choice.

1. A good team player _____
   - is convincing.
   - is an active listener.
   - is a great communicator.
   - is open-minded.

2. A successful teammate _____
   - takes initiative.
   - thinks others' ideas are better than hers/his.
   - is encouraging even when not honest.
   - is approachable.

3. Good teammates_____
   - do not talk about their personal lives.
   - do not show how they really feel.
   - identify themselves with their jobs.
   - are not critical of others.

34. GRAMMAR AND WRITING

Change the following verbs into adjectives. Use them to describe people in complete sentences. Follow the example.

1. COLLABORATE—COLLABORATIVE
   A collaborative person works willingly with others.

2. CONVINCE
   _____

3. ENCOURAGE
   _____

4. APPROACH
   _____

5. ACCEPT
   _____

35. SPEAKING

Discuss in groups. Take notes during your discussion.

1. Does everybody enjoy team work?
2. When do we need to perform tasks on our own?
3. Can you be a successful student if you are not a team player?
4. Can you be a successful employee if you are not a team player?
5. Describe a person who loves to work with others.
6. Describe a person who dislikes working with others.
7. Can you learn to like collaborative work?
8. Is society kind to individualists?
9. Why is collaboration an important skill in life?
10. Is progress possible without collaboration?

36. ESSAY WRITING

This activity is for everyone who wants to practice thinking and writing clearly. You can use all previous notes and write an essay in which you discuss collaboration skills. You can follow the guiding steps provided below.

	COLLABORATION SKILLS
ONE	Write an introduction in which you point out the importance of collaboration skills at school, at work, and social life in general.
TWO	Write a paragraph in which you discuss the significance of *collaboration skills at school*. In addition, show how we can develop them. Give examples of situations in which collaboration skills offer huge benefits.
THREE	Write a paragraph in which you discuss the importance of *collaboration skills at work*. In addition, indicate how we can improve them. Give examples of situations in which these skills offer numerous gains.
FOUR	Write a paragraph in which you discuss why some people might find it hard to collaborate with others. Give examples and explanations why *individual work* is sometimes beneficial.
FIVE	Write a conclusion in which you discuss how important collaboration is in all spheres of life.

OBSERVATION

37. SPEAKING

a. In groups, discuss the questions below. Take notes during your discussion.

1. What makes us pay attention to something?
2. What makes us pay attention to somebody?
3. Describe a person who is attentive.
4. Describe a person who is on guard.
5. What is the difference between attention and curiosity?
6. Does being observant mean being interested?
7. Give examples of situations when observation skills are imperative at school.
8. Give examples of situations when observation skills are significant in the workplace.
9. Does observation lead to new knowledge? Explain with examples.
10. How can we become good observers?

b. Rank the five alternatives according to their importance. In groups, give reasons for your ranking.

An excellent observer

- ☐ is alert to his/her surroundings.
- ☐ is genuinely interested in other people.
- ☐ is interested in self-improvement.
- ☐ wants to learn from people's behaviors.
- ☐ is curious.

c. **Answer the following questions with Yes or No. Explain your answers to a partner or in groups.**

AM I A GREAT OBSERVER IF:

- ☐ I am mindful of my surroundings?
- ☐ I am exclusively focused on what I feel and think?
- ☐ I easily identify a person's feelings of dissatisfaction?
- ☐ I fail to notice when somebody is frustrated?
- ☐ I feel that certain things were left out?
- ☐ I always make eye contact and read facial expressions?
- ☐ I have a great memory?
- ☐ I always try to make sense of my experiences?
- ☐ I connect present situations with earlier experiences?
- ☐ I get distracted by small details?

d. **Use a dictionary to answer the questions below.**

1. What are the typical attitudes of good observers? Make a list of adjectives to describe them.
2. What are the typical behaviors of good observers? Make a list of verbs to describe them.

38. WRITING

a. **Write a paragraph in which you discuss some ways to improve observation skills. Begin your paragraph with the topic sentence suggested below.**

There are diverse ways you can use to improve your observation skills.

b. **Write a paragraph in which you discuss the importance of observation skills in different domains of life. Begin your paragraph with the topic sentence suggested below.**

Clearly, observation skills are important in all spheres of life.

39. SPEAKING

Complete each statement with one of the alternatives provided. In groups, give reasons for your choice.

1. A good observer _____
   - is detail-oriented.
   - is good at reading body language.
   - is an active listener.
   - tries to see more than meets the eye.

2. A successful observer _____
   - notices unusual details.
   - is a successful leader.
   - recognizes repeated behavior.
   - focuses on others rather oneself.

3. Good observers_____
   - do not trust their own impressions.
   - trust their own impressions.
   - trust their eyes more than their ears.
   - trust their feelings more than their reason.

40. GRAMMAR AND WRITING

Change the following nouns into adjectives. Use them to describe people in complete sentences. Follow the example.

1. VIGILANCE—VIGILANT
   A vigilant person is watchful of possible difficult situations.

2. ATTENTION
   _____

3. IMPRESSION
   _____

4. CONSIDERATION
_____

5. EXPLORATION
_____

41. SPEAKING

Discuss in groups. Take notes during your discussion.

1. What is the difference between systematic and casual observation?
2. Give examples of work situations in which observation is critical.
3. Is the role of an observer a passive role?
4. What are some techniques of observing oneself?
5. What makes observing others different from self-observation?
6. Is self-observation possible without other people present?
7. Is self-improvement possible without self-observation?
8. Does one perform better or worse when one is being observed?
9. What distinguishes an observant from an unobservant learner?
10. Are problem solving skills possible without observation skills?

42. ESSAY WRITING

This activity is for everyone who wants to practice thinking and writing clearly. You can use all previous notes and write an essay in which you discuss observation skills. You can follow the guiding steps provided below.

	OBSERVATION SKILLS
ONE	Write an introduction in which you point out the importance of observation skills at school, at work, and social life in general.
TWO	Write a paragraph in which you discuss the significance of *observation skills at school*. In addition, show how we can develop them. Give examples of situations in which observation skills offer huge benefits.
THREE	Write a paragraph in which you discuss the importance of *observation skills at work*. In addition, indicate how we can improve them. Give examples of situations in which these skills offer numerous gains.
FOUR	Write a paragraph in which you discuss why some people might find it hard to observe themselves and others. Give examples and explanations why *observation should be practiced* deliberately and systematically in order to make them part of your skill set.
FIVE	Write a conclusion in which you discuss how important observation is in all spheres of life.

RESPONSIBILITY

43. SPEAKING

a. In groups, discuss the questions below. Take notes during your discussion.

1. What is personal responsibility?
2. What is social responsibility?
3. What is corporate responsibility?
4. What is moral responsibility?
5. Is being responsible the same as trustworthy?
6. Is responsibility different from guilt?
7. What is the relation between responsibility and choice?
8. Is responsibility and duty the same thing?
9. Do all jobs come with responsibilities?
10. Does everything in life come with responsibilities?

b. Rank the five alternatives according to their importance. In groups, give reasons for your ranking.

Responsible individuals

☐ are aware of their duties and obligations.
☐ are in control of their emotions.
☐ understand that all actions have consequences.
☐ never blame others for their own choices.
☐ always keep their promises.

c. **Answer the following questions with Yes or No. Explain your answers to a partner or in groups.**

AM I A RESPONSIBLE PERSON IF:

- ☐ I do not believe in free will?
- ☐ I obey authorities without thinking why?
- ☐ I find excuses for my mistakes?
- ☐ I take the blame for everything I do?
- ☐ I never take the blame for my actions?
- ☐ I believe actions are more important than intentions?
- ☐ I believe intentions are more important than actions?
- ☐ I always try to help people who experience misfortunes?
- ☐ I think I must contribute to a better world through small actions?
- ☐ I believe my family is more important than my community?

d. **Use a dictionary to answer the questions below.**

1. What are the typical attitudes of responsible people? Make a list of adjectives to describe them.
2. What are the typical behaviors of responsible people? Make a list of verbs to describe them.

44. WRITING

a. **Write a paragraph in which you discuss some ways to become a more responsible individual. Begin your paragraph with the topic sentence suggested below.**

There are many habits you can form to improve your responsibility skills.

b. **Write a paragraph in which you discuss the importance of responsibility in different domains of life. Begin your paragraph with the topic sentence suggested below.**

Clearly, responsibility skills are important in all spheres of life.

45. SPEAKING

Complete each statement with one of the alternatives provided. In groups, give reasons for your choice.

1. A responsible worker _____
   - is a good team player.
   - performs duties diligently.
   - takes charge of difficult situations.
   - is never late.

2. A responsible person _____
   - controls her emotions.
   - takes care of everybody around them.
   - blames himself for everything.
   - focuses on others rather oneself.

3. Responsible persons_____
   - do not trust words but actions.
   - trust themselves more than others.
   - trust others more than themselves.
   - trust their feelings more than their reason.

46. GRAMMAR AND WRITING

Change the following nouns into adjectives. Use them to describe people in complete sentences. Follow the example.

1. TRUSTWORTHINESS—TRUSTWORTHY
   A trustworthy person is somebody you can always rely on.

2. BLAME
   _____

3. ACCOUNTABILITY
   _____

4. LOYALTY
_____

5. STABILITY
_____

47. SPEAKING

Discuss in groups. Take notes during your discussion.

1. What makes a company responsible?
2. What makes an employee responsible?
3. What makes a citizen responsible?
4. What makes a parent responsible?
5. What makes a student responsible?
6. Are we always responsible?
7. Is responsibility the same as duty?
8. Does not knowing absolve you of responsibility?
9. Are you responsible for the wrongdoings you witness?
10. Are you responsible for other people's feelings?

48. ESSAY WRITING

This activity is for everyone who wants to practice thinking and writing clearly. You can use all previous notes and write an essay in which you discuss responsibility. You can follow the guiding steps provided below.

	RESPONSIBILITY SKILLS
ONE	Write an introduction in which you point out the importance of taking responsibility at school, at work, and social life in general.
TWO	Write a paragraph in which you discuss the significance of *responsibility skills at school*. In addition, show how we can develop them. Give examples of situations in which responsibility skills offer huge benefits.
THREE	Write a paragraph in which you discuss the importance of *responsibility skills at work*. In addition, indicate how we can improve them. Give examples of situations in which these skills offer numerous gains.
FOUR	Write a paragraph in which you discuss why some people might find it hard to take responsibility. Give examples and explanations why *responsibility should be practiced* deliberately and systematically to make it part of your skill set.
FIVE	Write a conclusion in which you discuss how important responsibility is in all spheres of life.

PROBLEM SOLVING

49. SPEAKING

a. In groups, discuss the questions below. Take notes during your discussion.

1. Describe a person who never sees problems but only solutions.
2. What are typical ways to address a problem?
3. What are the main qualities of a problem solver?
4. How is solving a mathematics problem different from a puzzle?
5. What kinds of working situations need problem solving skills?
6. What kinds of learning situations need problem solving skills?
7. Does a problem solver listen or speak more?
8. Does a problem solver think or act more?
9. Is being creative[1] more important than being analytical[2]?
10. How does a problem solver handle stress?

b. Rank the five alternatives according to their importance. In groups, give reasons for your ranking.

An excellent problem solver

☐ anticipates problems.
☐ is very perceptive.
☐ is a fast thinker.
☐ is logical and organized.
☐ can see the bigger picture.

---

1 Imaginative, resourceful, innovative, ingenious
2 Systematic, logical, meticulous, organized

c. **Answer the following questions with Yes or No. Explain your answers to a partner or in groups.**

AM I A PROFICIENT PROBLEM SOLVER IF:

- ☐ I refuse to believe that not all problems have solutions?
- ☐ I get easily emotional?
- ☐ I am not good at socializing and have a reserved personality?
- ☐ I ask many questions and have few answers?
- ☐ I have many answers and ask few questions?
- ☐ I can easily anticipate problems?
- ☐ I like to be and work alone?
- ☐ I am an active listener and not a talker?
- ☐ I am spontaneous and do not like schedules?
- ☐ I care about the results and not the process?

d. **Consult a dictionary to answer the questions below.**

1. What are the typical attitudes of good problem solvers? Make a list of adjectives to describe them.
2. What are the typical behaviors of good problem solvers? Make a list of verbs to describe them.

50. WRITING

a. **Write a paragraph in which you discuss some ways to improve problem solving skills. Begin your paragraph with the topic sentence suggested below.**

There are different ways you can use to improve your problem solving skills.

b. **Write a paragraph in which you discuss the importance of problem solving skills in different domains of life. Begin your paragraph with the topic sentence suggested below.**

Clearly, problem solving skills are important in all spheres of life.

51. SPEAKING

Complete each statement with one of the alternatives provided (there is no right answer!). In groups, give reasons for your choice.

1. Problem solving people _____
- are very smart.
- like problems.
- are good researchers.
- are good at analyzing data.

2. A problem solving person _____
- is spontaneous.
- is creative.
- is organized.
- is sloppy.

3. Problem solving people _____
- never stop thinking.
- believe that no problems lack solutions.
- are optimists.
- rapidly identify relevant from irrelevant.

52. GRAMMAR AND WRITING

Change the following adjectives into verbs. Use them to describe people in complete sentences. Follow the example.

1. CREATIVE—CREATE
   A problem-solving person creates new solutions to difficult problems.

2. EXPERIMENTAL
   _____

3. INVENTIVE
   _____

4. EXPLANATORY
_____

5. IMAGINATIVE
_____

53. SPEAKING

1. Is a creative solution different from a practical solution?
2. As a problem solver, do you use critical or creative thinking?
3. Does problem solving require imagination or expertise?
4. Are problem solving skills based on invention or evaluation?
5. Is a problem solving person calculated or spontaneous?
6. Is being spontaneous the same as effective?
7. Is being flexible the same as open-minded?
8. When are problems opportunities?
9. Can anyone learn to be good at problem solving?
10. Do all problems have solutions?

54. ESSAY WRITING

This activity is for everyone who wants to practice thinking and writing clearly. You can use all previous notes and write an essay in which you discuss problem solving skills. You can follow the guiding steps provided below.

	PROBLEM SOLVING SKILLS
ONE	Write an introduction in which you point out the importance of problem solving skills at school, at work, and social life in general.
TWO	Write a paragraph in which you discuss the significance of *problem solving skills at school*. In addition, show how we can develop them. Give examples of situations in which problem solving skills offer huge benefits.
THREE	Write a paragraph in which you discuss the importance of *problem solving skills at work*. In addition, indicate how we can improve them. Give examples of situations in which these skills offer numerous gains.
FOUR	Write a paragraph in which you discuss why sometimes it may be hard to find solutions to problems. Offer some suggestions of how one can deal with situations when one cannot solve the problems oneself.
FIVE	Write a conclusion in which you discuss how important problem solving is in all spheres of life.

CONFLICT MANAGEMENT

55. SPEAKING

a. **In groups, discuss the questions below. Take notes during your discussion.**

1. When do conflicts arise?
2. What are common conflicts in the workplace?
3. What are common family conflicts?
4. What are common conflicts between friends?
5. What is the difference between a conflict and a disagreement?
6. What are common ways to resolve a conflict?
7. Describe a confrontational person.
8. Describe a person skillful in managing conflicts.
9. Are conflict management skills based on tolerance or empathy?
10. Can anyone learn conflict management skills?

b. **Rank the five alternatives according to their importance. In groups, give reasons for your ranking.**

An excellent conflict manager

☐ has great written and verbal communication skills.
☐ is emotionally intelligent.
☐ has great empathy skills.
☐ is good at making rules for productive dialogues.
☐ finds it easy to compromise.

c. Answer the following questions with Yes or No. Explain your answers to a partner or in groups.

AM I GOOD AT MANAGING CONFLICTS IF:

- ☐ I believe rules are more important than people?
- ☐ I think there is only one absolute truth?
- ☐ I am willing to change my opinion in light of new information?
- ☐ I always give the opposing side what it wants?
- ☐ I ignore or delay dealing with emerging conflicts?
- ☐ I find a solution agreeable for the powerful party?
- ☐ I give up my own interests in favor of my opponent?
- ☐ I think being correct is more important than being nice?
- ☐ I always compromise because I am afraid of confrontation?
- ☐ I do not get emotionally involved and keep a cool head?

d. Consult a dictionary to answer the questions below.

1. What are the typical attitudes of good conflict managers? Make a list of adjectives to describe them.
2. What are the typical behaviors of good conflict managers? Make a list of verbs to describe them.

56. WRITING

a. Write a paragraph in which you discuss some ways to improve conflict management skills. Begin your paragraph with the topic sentence suggested below.

There are different ways you can use to become skillful at resolving conflicts.

b. Write a paragraph in which you discuss the importance of conflict management skills in different domains of life. Begin your paragraph with the topic sentence suggested below.

Clearly, conflict management skills are important in all spheres of life.

CONFLICT MANAGEMENT

57. SPEAKING

Complete each statement with one of the alternatives provided (there is no right answer!). In groups, give reasons for your choice.

1. People who manage conflicts well _____
   - are on good terms with everyone.
   - dislike problems.
   - are good negotiators.
   - are willing to change behavior.

2. A great conflict manager _____
   - is forgiving.
   - is creative.
   - is emotional.
   - is adaptable.

3. Great conflict managers _____
   - handle negative feelings well.
   - believe that reason should prevail over emotions.
   - are active listeners.
   - are the best employees.

58. GRAMMAR AND WRITING

Change the following nouns into adjectives. Use them to describe people in complete sentences. Follow the example.

1. AGRESSION—AGGRESSIVE
   An aggressive person is hostile and violent.

2. ANTAGONISM
   _____

3. CONFRONTATION
   _____

4. QUARREL

_____

5. OFFENSE

_____

59. SPEAKING

1. When should one put up a fight?
2. Is compromise always the solution?
3. Is being understanding the same as empathetic?
4. Is a conflict of opinion different from a conflict of interest?
5. Can you be a good employee without conflict management skills?
6. Is a conflict-free workplace possible?
7. Is a conflict-free world possible?
8. Can conflicts ever be useful?
9. Can conflicts be solved without compromise?
10. Does understanding guarantee conflict resolution?

60. ESSAY WRITING

This activity is for everyone who wants to practice thinking and writing clearly. You can use all previous notes and write an essay in which you discuss conflict management skills. You can follow the guiding steps provided below.

	CONFLICT MANAGEMENT SKILLS
ONE	Write an introduction in which you point out the importance of conflict management skills at school, at work, and social life in general.
TWO	Write a paragraph in which you discuss the significance of *conflict management skills in all kinds of life situations*. In addition, show how we can develop them. Give examples of situations in which conflict management skills offer huge benefits.
THREE	Write a paragraph in which you discuss the importance of *conflict management skills at work*. In addition, indicate how we can improve them. Give examples of situations in which these skills offer numerous gains.
FOUR	Write a paragraph in which you discuss why sometimes it may be hard to resolve conflicts. Offer some solutions of how one can deal with situations when one cannot resolve certain conflicts alone.
FIVE	Write a conclusion in which you discuss how important conflict management is in all spheres of life.

CRITICAL THINKING

61. SPEAKING

a. In groups, discuss the questions below. Take notes during your discussion.

1. What makes us seek information?
2. When and why do we analyze data and information?
3. What skills do we use to differentiate between relevant and irrelevant facts?
4. How do we transform our present knowledge into new knowledge?
5. How do we predict outcomes and why is it an important skill?
6. What is the difference between describing and discussing something?
7. What is the difference between being critical and thinking critically?
8. What is the difference between reflection and self-reflection?
9. What makes you decide that something is more important than something else?
10. Is knowing something the same as understanding it?

b. Rank the five alternatives according to their importance. In groups, give reasons for your ranking.

An excellent critical thinker

- ☐ analyzes old information in light of new data.
- ☐ recognizes logical connections between ideas.
- ☐ distinguishes relevant ideas and sources from irrelevant ones.
- ☐ reflects over the reasons for her/his own values and beliefs.
- ☐ identifies, evaluates and builds arguments.

132 SKILLS: A PRACTICAL GUIDE IN CONVERSATION, VOCABULARY AND WRITING

c. Answer the following questions with Yes or No. Explain your answers to a partner or in groups.

AM I A SUCCESSFUL CRITICAL THINKER IF:

- ☐ I accept things at face value?
- ☐ I am humble and know that there is a lot I don't know?
- ☐ I am confident in my beliefs and values?
- ☐ I over-think everything?
- ☐ I see how details make up the bigger picture?
- ☐ I read many books but have no opinion about them?
- ☐ I know a lot of facts and am good at accumulating information?
- ☐ I am argumentative and critical of other people?
- ☐ I integrate different sources of information into solving problems?
- ☐ I evaluate ideas and generate new ones?

d. Use a dictionary to answer the questions below.

1. What are the typical abilities of a critical thinker? Make a list of nouns to identify them.
2. What are the typical behaviors of a person willing to change her/his mind when presented with new information/arguments? Make a list of verbs to describe them.

62. WRITING

a. Write a paragraph in which you discuss some ways to improve critical thinking skills. Begin your paragraph with the topic sentence suggested below.

There are different ways you can use to improve your critical thinking skills.

b. Write a paragraph in which you discuss the importance of critical thinking skills in different domains of life. Begin your paragraph with the topic sentence suggested below.

Clearly, critical thinking skills are important in all spheres of life.

63. SPEAKING

Complete each statement with one of the alternatives provided. In groups, give reasons for your choice.

1. An excellent critical thinker _____
   - is logical.
   - is a fast thinker.
   - is intellectually disciplined.
   - is good at processing information.

2. An outstanding critical thinker _____
   - makes connections between ideas.
   - has a sharp mind.
   - is nonconformist.
   - is very creative.

3. Great critical thinkers_____
   - stop and think deliberately.
   - are always ready to explain their views.
   - are self-aware.
   - are critical of everything

64. GRAMMAR AND WRITING

Change the following verbs into adjectives. Use them to describe people in complete sentences. Follow the example.

1. ANALYZE—ANALYTICAL
   An analytical person uses methodical and logical reasoning.

2. INQUIRE
   _____

3. EVALUATE
   _____

4. INVESTIGATE
_____

5. SYSTEMATIZE
_____

65. SPEAKING

Discuss in groups. Take notes during your discussion.

1. What is the difference between automatic and deliberate thinking?
2. What makes critical thinking essential in the workplace?
3. Describe a person with an inquisitive mind.
4. Is an adult inquisitive in the same way a child is?
5. Can you become a good critical thinker without discipline?
6. Do emotions hinder or facilitate critical thinking?
7. Do we think critically when we think subjectively?
8. Is objective thinking possible?
9. What is the relation between knowledge and experience?
10. What makes critical thinking vital in life?

66. ESSAY WRITING

This activity is for everyone who wants to practice thinking and writing clearly. You can use all previous notes and write an essay in which you discuss critical thinking skills. You can follow the guiding steps provided below.

	CRITICAL THINKING SKILLS
ONE	Write an introduction in which you point out the importance of critical thinking skills at school, at work, and life in general.
TWO	Write a paragraph in which you discuss the significance of *critical thinking skills at school*. In addition, show how we can develop them. Give examples of situations in which critical thinking offers huge benefits.
THREE	Write a paragraph in which you discuss the importance of *critical thinking at work*. In addition, indicate how we can improve them. Give examples of situations in which these skills offer numerous gains.
FOUR	Write a paragraph in which you discuss why some people might find it hard to think critically. Give examples and explanations how today's world poses many critical thinking challenges.
FIVE	Write a conclusion in which you discuss how important critical thinking is in all spheres of life.

SELF-MOTIVATION

67. SPEAKING

a. In groups, discuss the questions below. Take notes during your discussion.

1. What makes people want to do things?
2. What makes people challenge themselves?
3. What makes people avoid challenges?
4. What are some forms of self-assessment?
5. Is personal growth different from professional growth?
6. How do employers make employees motivated?
7. How do employers fail to motivate their employees?
8. Are you a good worker if you do not want to go the extra mile?
9. What is the role of feedback in self-motivation?
10. Is self-motivation a skill everybody can learn?

b. Rank the five alternatives according to their importance. In groups, give reasons for your ranking.

A self-motivated person

☐ sets high but realistic goals for herself/himself.
☐ deals successfully with setbacks and criticism.
☐ takes initiative and makes more efforts than required.
☐ reflects over her/his own work and how it can be improved.
☐ identifies problems and tries hard to find solutions.

c. Answer the following questions with Yes or No. Explain your answers to a partner or in groups.

AM I ADEPT AT SELF-MOTIVATION IF:

- ☐ I perform tasks only because they are part of my job?
- ☐ I do not think it is crucial to improve my performance at work?
- ☐ I am confident I always do a good job?
- ☐ I believe intrinsic motivators should top extrinsic motivators?
- ☐ I believe extrinsic motivators should overshadow intrinsic motivators?
- ☐ I always do the minimum necessary and relax the rest of my time?
- ☐ I am always ready to act on new opportunities?
- ☐ I am open to feedback and try to learn new things every day?
- ☐ I see life as a continuous educational journey?
- ☐ I regularly examine my own learning and performance?

d. Consult a dictionary to answer the questions below.

1. What are the typical attitudes of a self-motivated person? Make a list of adjectives to describe them.
2. What are the typical behaviors of a self-motivated person? Make a list of verbs to describe them.

68. WRITING

a. Write a paragraph in which you discuss some ways to improve self-motivation skills. Begin your paragraph with the topic sentence suggested below.

There are different ways you can use to improve your self-motivation skills.

b. Write a paragraph in which you discuss the importance of self-motivation skills in different domains of life. Begin your paragraph with the topic sentence suggested below.

Clearly, self-motivation skills are important in all spheres of life.

SELF-MOTIVATION

69. SPEAKING

Complete each statement with one of the alternatives provided. In groups, give reasons for your choice.

1. An excellent self-motivated person _____
   - is not afraid to ask questions.
   - is very ambitious.
   - has a strong willpower.
   - transforms mistakes into lessons.

2. An outstanding self-motivated person _____
   - is very disciplined.
   - believes in the power of hard work.
   - is passionate about her/his job.
   - is very inventive.

3. Highly self-motivated people _____
   - have high expectations of themselves.
   - have high expectations of others.
   - are great decision-makers.
   - are self-critical.

70. GRAMMAR AND WRITING

Change the following nouns into verbs. Use them to describe people in complete sentences. Follow the example.

1. IMPROVEMENT—IMPROVE
   A self-motivated person tries to improve herself all the time.

2. REFLECTION
   _____

3. DRIVE
   _____

4. GROWTH
_____

5. COMMITMENT
_____

71. SPEAKING

Discuss in groups. Take notes during your discussion.

1. Is social comparison beneficial?
2. Is professional comparison beneficial?
3. Is continuous self-improvement necessary?
4. What is personal fulfilment?
5. What is professional fulfilment?
6. Is self-motivation more important for personal or professional success?
7. Is there a job for every person in the world to love?
8. Why is it important to know your strengths and weaknesses?
9. What is the relation between self-knowledge and self-improvement?
10. Why are people afraid of change?

72. ESSAY WRITING

This activity is for everyone who wants to practice thinking and writing clearly. You can use all previous notes and write an essay in which you discuss self-motivation skills. You can follow the guiding steps provided below.

	SELF-MOTIVATION SKILLS
ONE	Write an introduction in which you point out the importance of self-motivation skills at school, at work, and life in general.
TWO	Write a paragraph in which you discuss the significance of *self-motivation skills at school*. In addition, show how we can develop them. Give examples of situations in which self-motivation offers huge benefits.
THREE	Write a paragraph in which you discuss the importance of *self-motivation skills at work*. In addition, indicate how we can improve them. Give examples of situations in which these skills offer numerous gains.
FOUR	Write a paragraph in which you discuss why some people might find it hard to motivate themselves and take initiative to do things. Give examples and explanations how today's world needs people able to motivate and improve themselves on their own.
FIVE	Write a conclusion in which you discuss how important self-motivation is in all spheres of life.

DIGITAL COMPETENCE

73. SPEAKING

  a. **In groups, discuss the questions below. Take notes during your discussion.**

  1. What is information and why do we need it?
  2. What are digital technologies and why do we need them?
  3. What are some ways of searching information?
  4. What are some ways of processing information?
  5. What is digital content and who can create it?
  6. What is digital safety and why is it vital?
  7. How do we communicate with other people today?
  8. What are some routine problems digital electronics pose?
  9. What are the benefits of digital technologies?
  10. Is digital competence easy or difficult to learn?

  b. **Rank the five alternatives according to their importance. In groups, give reasons for your ranking.**

  A digitally competent person

  ☐ performs tasks efficiently in a digital setting.
  ☐ reads and interprets media rapidly and successfully.
  ☐ recreates data and images by digital manipulation.
  ☐ creates new knowledge from different reliable sources.
  ☐ is able to instantly process and assess great amounts of information.

c. **Answer the following questions with Yes or No. Explain your answers to a partner or in groups.**

AM I A DIGITALLY COMPETENT PERSON IF:

- ☐ I use software to organize large volumes of information when I study and work?
- ☐ I interact with family, friends, and colleagues in real time via my mobile phone?
- ☐ I use my mobile to clarify words and concepts when I read?
- ☐ I am rarely sure whether what I am reading is true or not?
- ☐ I make use of technologies to verify and compare information?
- ☐ I use daily different social media and platforms of communication?
- ☐ I tend to click on links sent from senders unknown to me?
- ☐ I feel overwhelmed by the flow of information and use technology minimally?
- ☐ I am rarely aware of how much private information I offer when I log on new websites?
- ☐ I easily switch between tasks on different gadgets?

d. **Consult a dictionary to answer the questions below.**

1. What are the typical abilities of a digitally literate person? Make a list of nouns to designate them.
2. What are the typical behaviors of a digitally literate person? Make a list of verbs to describe them.

74. WRITING

a. **Write a paragraph in which you discuss some ways to improve digital skills. Begin your paragraph with the topic sentence suggested below.**

There are different ways you can use to improve your digital skills.

b. Write a paragraph in which you discuss the importance of digital skills in different domains of modern life. Begin your paragraph with the topic sentence suggested below.

Clearly, digital skills are important in all spheres of life in the modern world.

75. SPEAKING

Complete each statement with one of the alternatives provided. In groups, give reasons for your choice.

1. A digital competent person _____
   - uses technology daily.
   - is aware of information sources.
   - can easily locate and access data.
   - spends a lot of time online.

2. A digitally literate person _____
   - fails to evaluate the quality of information.
   - uses technology to interact with coworkers.
   - uses technology to perform better at work.
   - is active on social media.

3. Digitally skilled persons _____
   - believe mobile phones hinder learning.
   - believe mobile phones facilitate learning.
   - are great critical thinkers.
   - use digital technologies to solve problems.

76. GRAMMAR AND WRITING

Change the following adjectives into verbs. Use them to describe people in complete sentences. Follow the example.

1. STORED—STORE
   A digitally skilled person knows where and how to store and retrieve information.

2. INTERACTIVE

3. RESPONSIVE

4. REVIEWED

5. EVALUATED

77. SPEAKING

Discuss in groups. Take notes during your discussion.

1. What makes cyberbullying different from face-to-face bullying?
2. What makes critical thinking closely connected to digital skills?
3. What are the benefits of digital technologies?
4. What are the challenges of digital technologies?
5. Do you feel safer in online or offline communication?
6. Has technology increased or decreased inequality worldwide?
7. Has technology increased or decreased human understanding?
8. Has technology made learning and work more meaningful?
9. Why does digital interaction cause anxiety?
10. How can digital interaction contribute to a better life?

78. ESSAY WRITING

This activity is for everyone who wants to practice thinking and writing clearly. You can use all previous notes and write an essay in which you discuss digital skills. You can follow the guiding steps provided below.

	DIGITAL SKILLS
ONE	Write an introduction in which you point out the importance of digital skills at school, at work, and life in general.
TWO	Write a paragraph in which you discuss the significance of *digital skills at school*. In addition, show how we can develop them. Give examples of situations in which digital competence offers huge benefits.
THREE	Write a paragraph in which you discuss the importance of *digital skills at work*. In addition, indicate how we can improve them. Give examples of situations in which these skills offer numerous gains.
FOUR	Write a paragraph in which you discuss why some people might find it hard to deal with the challenges and frustrations that the digital world presents. Give examples and explanations how today's world requires skills to identify and evaluate data and information online, and use that for self-improvement.
FIVE	Write a conclusion in which you discuss how significant digital competence is in all spheres of the modern life.

EMOTIONAL INTELLIGENCE

79. SPEAKING

a. In groups, discuss the questions below. Take notes during your discussion.

1. Are you always aware of how you feel?
2. Are you always aware of how others feel?
3. What does putting yourself in another's place mean?
4. What is the difference between sympathy and empathy?
5. When are empathy skills crucial at school?
6. When are empathy skills crucial at work?
7. When are emotions more important than reason?
8. When is reason more important than emotions?
9. How can we apply emotions to problem solving tasks?
10. What are the best ways to manage our emotions?

b. Rank the five alternatives according to their importance. In groups, give reasons for your ranking.

An emotionally intelligent person

- ☐ identifies easily her/his emotions and controls them.
- ☐ registers others' feelings.
- ☐ reads nonverbal communication.
- ☐ is good at taming negative feelings.
- ☐ is adept at handling various types of relationships.

c. **Answer the following questions with Yes or No. Explain your answers to a partner or in groups.**

AM I AN EMOTIONALLY INTELLIGENT PERSON IF:

- ☐ I seldom think about the causes of my emotions?
- ☐ I get angry easily and lash out?
- ☐ I trust my intuition and make decisions based on it?
- ☐ I adjust my message to different people in accordance with their attitudes?
- ☐ I know exactly what to say and how in different circumstances?
- ☐ I ask questions when I feel that the other person is aloof?
- ☐ I see my own fears in others and find discomfort in it?
- ☐ I see my own fears in others and find comfort in it?
- ☐ I feel often overwhelmed by anxiety and analyze its causes by discussing it with others?
- ☐ I become distressed when I see people in distress?

d. **Consult a dictionary to answer the questions below.**

1. What are the typical attitudes of an emotionally intelligent person? Make a list of adjectives to describe them.
2. What are the typical behaviors of an emotionally intelligent person? Make a list of verbs to describe them.

80. WRITING

a. **Write a paragraph in which you discuss some ways to improve emotional competence. Begin your paragraph with the topic sentence suggested below.**

There are different ways you can use to improve your emotional intelligence.

b. Write a paragraph in which you discuss the importance of emotional competence in different domains of life today. Begin your paragraph with the topic sentence suggested below.

Clearly, emotional intelligence is important in all spheres of life.

81. SPEAKING

Complete each statement with one of the alternatives provided. In groups, give reasons for your choice.

1. An emotionally intelligent person _____
   - is self-ware.
   - is in control of emotions and impulses.
   - is very likeable.
   - spends time analyzing others' behaviors.

2. Emotionally intelligent people _____
   - react calmly to stressful situations.
   - believe emotions are more important than reason.
   - are great team players.
   - use others' emotions to achieve their goals.

3. Emotionally intelligent persons _____
   - react with anger to unfair situations.
   - are trustworthy classmates/colleagues.
   - are too trusting.
   - have great conflict management skills.

82. GRAMMAR AND WRITING

Change the following nouns into adjectives. Use them to describe people in complete sentences. Follow the example.

1. AWARENESS—AWARE
   An emotionally intelligent person is aware of her own feelings and those of others.

2. MANAGEMENT
   _____

3. ADAPTABILITY
   _____

4. UNDERSTANDING
   _____

5. EMPATHY
   _____

83. SPEAKING

Discuss in groups. Take notes during your discussion.

1. Should negative emotions be contained rather than expressed?
2. Should we always trust our emotions?
3. When are emotions our friends?
4. When are emotions our foes?
5. What is the relation between self-control and success?
6. What makes emotional awareness the core of human relationships?
7. How does understanding yourself help you understand others?
8. What makes self-regulation extremely important in the workplace?
9. Can personal relationships be enjoyable without empathy?
10. Can professional relationships be rewarding without empathy?

84. ESSAY WRITING

This activity is for everyone who wants to practice thinking and writing clearly. You can use all previous notes and write an essay in which you discuss emotional intelligence. You can follow the guiding steps provided below.

	EMOTIONAL INTELLIGENCE
ONE	Write an introduction in which you point out the importance of emotional intelligence at school, at work, and life in general.
TWO	Write a paragraph in which you discuss the significance of *emotional intelligence at school*. In addition, show how we can develop it. Give examples of situations in which emotional intelligence offers huge benefits.
THREE	Write a paragraph in which you discuss the importance of *emotional intelligence at work*. In addition, indicate how we can improve it. Give examples of situations in which these skills offer numerous gains.
FOUR	Write a paragraph in which you discuss why some people might find it hard to identify and adapt to their own and others' emotions. Give examples and explanations of why people need emotional intelligence for personal and professional fulfilment.
FIVE	Write a conclusion in which you discuss how significant emotional intelligence is in all spheres of life.

ETHICAL REASONING

85. SPEAKING

a. In groups, discuss the questions below. Take notes during your discussion.

1. How do we distinguish right from wrong?
2. Where do we learn to differentiate between right and wrong?
3. What is a moral dilemma?
4. What are typical moral dilemmas in personal relationships?
5. What are typical moral dilemmas in professional relationships?
6. What are typical moral dilemmas in learning situations?
7. Is keeping promises as important as coming on time?
8. Is being fair-minded different from being open-minded?
9. What is the difference between assumption and conclusion?
10. What is the difference between moral and non-moral behavior?

b. Rank the five alternatives according to their importance. In groups, give reasons for your ranking.

An effective ethical reasoner

- ☐ considers more than one side of the story.
- ☐ tests the trustworthiness of the position taken.
- ☐ identifies different conflicting values.
- ☐ is good at reflecting upon causes and effects.
- ☐ is adept at placing opinions and beliefs in context.

c. Answer the following questions with Yes or No. Explain your answers to a partner or in groups.

AM I A GOOD ETHICAL REASONER IF:

- ☐ I prefer fairness to kindness?
- ☐ I believe that the interests of many are greater than those of the few?
- ☐ I identify prejudicial attitudes easily and try to eliminate them?
- ☐ I trust my feelings when I make decisions affecting others?
- ☐ I anticipate consequences before I make decisions?
- ☐ I show respect even when I disagree?
- ☐ I believe justice is not the same as equality?
- ☐ I think intuition is the ultimate guide to moral behavior?
- ☐ I resort to rules and law when I am unsure what to do?
- ☐ I become angry when I feel offended?

d. Consult a dictionary to answer the questions below.

1. What are the typical attitudes of an effective ethical reasoner? Make a list of adjectives to describe them.
2. What are the typical behaviors of an effective ethical reasoner? Make a list of verbs to describe them.

86. WRITING

a. Write a paragraph in which you discuss some ways to improve ethical reasoning skills. Begin your paragraph with the topic sentence suggested below.

There are different ways you can use to improve your ethical reasoning skills.

b. Write a paragraph in which you discuss the importance of moral competence in different domains of life. Begin your paragraph with the topic sentence suggested below.

Clearly, ethical reasoning is important in all spheres of life.

87. SPEAKING

Complete each statement with one of the alternatives provided. In groups, give reasons for your choice.

1. An effective ethical reasoner _____
   - is objective and fair.
   - is in control of emotions and impulses.
   - is concerned with the well-being of others.
   - is concerned with actions rather than words.

2. People with excellent ethical reasoning skills _____
   - dedicate a lot of time to evaluating reasons.
   - believe moral decisions should be based on their outcomes.
   - believe moral decisions should be based on emotions.
   - believe it is easy to be right when you trust your intuition.

3. People good at ethical reasoning _____
   - put others' interests before their own.
   - believe compassion is more important than impartiality.
   - believe impartiality is more important than compassion.
   - have very rigid moral principles.

88. GRAMMAR AND WRITING

Change the following verbs into adjectives. Use them to describe people in complete sentences. Follow the example.

1. PACIFY—PACIFYING
   A pacifying person is good at reducing or avoiding conflicts and animosity.

2. EXPLORE
   _____

3. DECIDE
   _____

4. SELECT
_____

5. DETERMINE
_____

89. SPEAKING

Discuss in groups. Take notes during your discussion.

1. Should others' feelings count more than our own?
2. Should parents prioritize their children's happiness over their own?
3. Should we prioritize the community's interests over our family's?
4. Is being right the same as being fair?
5. Is being professional the same as competent?
6. Is being law-abiding the same as right-minded?
7. What is exemplary behavior in the workplace?
8. Is social life possible without ethical reasoning skills?
9. Is being honest as important as being kind?
10. What would a world without a moral compass look like?

90. ESSAY WRITING

This activity is for everyone who wants to practice thinking and writing clearly. You can use all previous notes and write an essay in which you discuss ethical reasoning skills. You can follow the guiding steps provided below.

	ETHICAL REASONING SKILLS
ONE	Write an introduction in which you point out the importance of ethical reasoning in relationships, in the workplace, and society in general.
TWO	Write a paragraph in which you discuss the significance of *ethical reasoning in relationships*. In addition, show how we can develop them. Give examples of situations in which moral decisions are fundamental.
THREE	Write a paragraph in which you discuss the importance of *ethical reasoning at work*. In addition, indicate how we can improve them. Give examples of situations in which these skills offer numerous gains.
FOUR	Write a paragraph in which you discuss some morally challenging situations in social life. Give examples and explanations of why people need ethical reasoning skills to navigate social life successfully.
FIVE	Write a conclusion in which you discuss how significant ethical reasoning is in all spheres of life.

CHAPTER 3

SKILLS AND JOBS

This chapter makes a connection between personal and general skills with different kinds of jobs. It also includes a great deal of research into a third type of skills—knowledge-based skills. It is important to point out that you are free to focus on other kinds of jobs should they be more relevant for you, and you can use the chapter activities as guidelines. This chapter is not meant to focus on specific jobs, but on specific ways to think about jobs in general.

HEALTHCARE

1. **RESEARCH**

    a. **Go online and find information which will help you answer the questions below.**

    1. What is healthcare?
    2. Who provides healthcare services?
    3. Who needs healthcare services?
    4. What are the differences between public and private sectors?
    5. What is preventive medicine?
    6. Do all countries have a free healthcare system?
    7. Should all countries have a free healthcare system?

    b. **In groups, discuss the questions above. Take notes during your discussion.**

    c. **Write a paragraph in which you summarize your research and discussion.**

2. **WHAT DOES A NURSE DO?**

    a. **In groups, discuss the questions below. Go online to find out more when necessary. Take notes during your discussion.**

    1. What are the required qualifications to become a registered nurse in your country?
    2. What is the knowledge required to work as a nurse?

3. What are the personal skills a nurse should have? Make a list.
4. What are the general skills a nurse should have? Make a list.

b. Write a paragraph in which you summarize your discussion.

c. In groups, describe the typical day of a nurse. In your description, include the words suggested below.

Morning rounds	Patient appointments and testing	Labor and delivery nurse
Afternoon rounds	Review charts	Pediatric nurse
Night shifts	Collect and record data	School nurse
Day shifts	Administer medication	Oncology nurse
Action-packed days	Review lab results	Staff nurse
Medical emergency	Handle emergencies	Nursing assistant
Patient assessment	Manage admissions and discharges	Home health nurse

d. Write a paragraph in which you summarize your discussion.

e. In groups, discuss the questions below. Explain your views and offer examples.

1. Should a nurse be more empathetic or more proactive?
2. Is self-sacrifice a fundamental skill in nursing?
3. Are you fit to work as a nurse if you are not detail oriented?
4. Can a nurse with no confidence do her job properly?
5. Do you need to be flexible when you work as a nurse?
6. What other personal skills should a nurse have?

f. **Write a paragraph in which you summarize your discussion.**

g. **In groups, discuss the questions below. Explain your views and offer examples.**

1. Is cooperation a more significant skill than communication for a nurse?
2. Is listening more important than speaking when you work as a nurse?
3. Should a nurse be better at managing conflicts rather than solving problems?
4. Is emotional intelligence at the heart of nursing?
5. Is ethical reasoning a skill all nurses must have?
6. What other general skills should a nurse have?

h. **Write a paragraph in which you summarize your discussion.**

3. WHAT DOES A PHYSICIAN DO?

a. **In groups, discuss the questions below. Go online to find out more when necessary. Take notes during your discussion.**

1. What are the required qualifications to become a physician in your country?
2. What is the knowledge required to work as a physician?
3. What are the personal skills a physician should possess? Make a list.
4. What are the general skills a physician should possess? Make a list.

b. **Write a paragraph in which you summarize your discussion.**

c. **In groups, describe a physician's typical day. In your description, include the words suggested below.**

Follow-ups	Consult patients	Medical practitioner
Clinic sessions	Address emergencies	General practitioner
Pre-op evaluation of patients	Confer with the medical team	Family physician
Post-operative visits	Prescribe medication	Neurologist
Night schedule	Discuss reports and labs	Surgeon
Call-backs	Make diagnoses	Cardiologist
Direct patient care	Update records	Dermatologist
Treatment recommendations	Review medical journals	Ophthalmologist

d. **Write a paragraph in which you summarize your discussion.**

e. **In groups, discuss the questions below. Explain your views and offer examples.**

1. Should physicians be more empathetic or more curious?
2. If you are not courageous, are you fit to be a physician?
3. Is confidence a skill or a weakness when you practice medicine?
4. Should a physician be more detail oriented or more sociable?
5. Can a doctor who is not passionate about her/his job be a competent doctor?
6. What other personal skills should a physician have?

f. **Write a paragraph in which you summarize your discussion.**

g. **In groups, discuss the questions below. Explain your views and offer examples.**

1. Are ethical reasoning skills the most important skills a physician must possess?

2. Should a physician listen more than speak, and write more than read?
3. As a physician, is it more important to be observant or to be communicative?
4. Does critical thinking lie at the heart of a physician's job?
5. If you are not a proficient problem solver, are you fit for practicing medicine?
6. What other general skills should a physician possess?

h. Write a paragraph in which you summarize your discussion.

4. RESEARCH

a. Go online and find information to answer the questions below.

1. Find at least two more jobs within healthcare.
2. What are the formal qualifications necessary to practice them?
3. What is the knowledge required to perform these jobs?
4. What are the personal skills necessary to do these jobs?
5. What are the general skills necessary for the jobs?

b. Share your findings in groups.

5. ESSAY WRITING

Use all previous notes and write an essay in which you discuss healthcare jobs and skills. You can follow the guiding instructions provided below. Remember to give your essay a title.

ONE	Write an introduction in which you point out the importance of healthcare jobs, and introduce one job you believe is the most significant for you or in general.
TWO	Write a paragraph in which you discuss the *qualifications and knowledge* necessary to perform this job. Give examples, explanations, and details.
THREE	Write a paragraph in which you discuss the *personal skills* necessary to perform this job. Give examples, explanations, and details.
FOUR	Write a paragraph in which you discuss the *general skills* necessary to perform this job. Give examples, explanations, and details.
FIVE	Write a conclusion in which you discuss how important this job and skills are for the social life.

MENTAL HEALTHCARE

6. RESEARCH

   a. **Go online and find information which will help you answer the questions below.**

   1. What is mental healthcare?
   2. What are mental health problems?
   3. What is the difference between depression and anxiety?
   4. What are the biggest causes of stress?
   5. What are eating disorders?
   6. Who provides mental healthcare services?
   7. Who needs mental healthcare services?

   b. **In groups, discuss the questions above. Take notes during your discussion.**

   c. **Write a paragraph in which you summarize your research and discussion.**

7. WHAT DOES A PSYCHOLOGIST DO?

   a. **In groups, discuss the questions below. Go online to find out more when necessary. Take notes during your discussion.**

   1. What are the required qualifications to become a psychologist in your country?
   2. What is the knowledge required to work as a psychologist?

3. What are the personal skills a psychologist should have? Make a list.
4. What are the general skills a psychologist should have? Make a list.

b. Write a paragraph in which you summarize your research and discussion.

c. In groups, describe a psychologist's typical day. In your description, include the words suggested below.

Team meetings	Evaluate individual problems	School psychologist
Professional consultations	Interview patients	Social psychologist
Staff meetings	Counsel people	Clinical psychologist
Documentation	Develop action plans	Criminal psychologist
Emotional energy	Identify mental needs	Child psychologist
Mental health	Make referrals to specialists	Sports psychologist
Treatment plans	Write psychological reports	Counseling psychologist

d. Write a paragraph in which you summarize your discussion.

e. In groups, discuss the questions below. Explain your views and offer examples.

1. Should a psychologist focus on details or the big picture?
2. Is empathy a fundamental skill for a psychologist?
3. Are you fit to work as a psychologist if you are not curious?
4. Can a psychologist with no social skills do her job properly?
5. Do you need to be passionate when you work as a psychologist?
6. What other personal skills should a psychologist have?

f. **Write a paragraph in which you summarize your research and discussion.**

g. **In groups, discuss the questions below. Explain your views and offer examples.**

1. Is observation a more significant skill than communication for a psychologist?
2. Should a psychologist speak more and listen less?
3. Should a psychologist be a better critical thinker rather than emotionally intelligent?
4. How important is self-motivation for a psychologist?
5. Is ethical reasoning a skill all psychologists must have?
6. What other general skills should a psychologist have?

h. **Write a paragraph in which you summarize your research and discussion.**

8. WHAT DOES A PSYCHIATRIST DO?

a. **In groups, discuss the questions below. Go online to find out more when necessary. Take notes during your discussion.**

1. What are the required qualifications to become a psychiatrist in your country?
2. What is the knowledge required to work as a psychiatrist?
3. What are the personal skills a psychiatrist should have? Make a list.
4. What are the general skills a psychiatrist should have? Make a list.

b. Write a paragraph in which you summarize your research and discussion.

c. In groups, describe a psychiatrist's typical day. In your description, include the words suggested below.

Office visits	Review diagnostic criteria	Addiction psychiatrist
Patient information and records	Prescribe psychotherapeutic treatments	Child and adolescent psychiatrist
Panic disorders		
Schizophrenia		
Cognitive dissonance	Treat emotional behaviors	Adult psychiatrist
Complains of depression	Treat behavioral disorders	Clinical psychiatrist
Preliminary interpretations	Analyze and evaluate patient data	Consulting psychiatrist
	Diagnose mental disorders	Behavioral analyst

d. Write a paragraph in which you summarize your discussion.

e. In groups, discuss the questions below. Explain your views and offer examples.

1. Should a psychiatrist be empathetic?
2. Is compassion more important than curiosity for a psychiatrist?
3. Are you fit to work as a psychiatrist if you are not patient?
4. Can a psychiatrist with no social skills do her job properly?
5. Do you need to be confident when you work as a psychiatrist?
6. What other personal skills should a psychiatrist have?

f. **Write a paragraph in which you summarize your research and discussion.**

g. **In groups, discuss the questions below. Explain your views and offer examples.**

1. Is communication a more significant skill than observation for a psychiatrist?
2. Can a psychiatrist do a good job if they are not active listeners?
3. How significant is responsibility for the job of the psychiatrist?
4. How important are problem solving skills for a psychiatrist?
5. Is critical thinking a skill all psychiatrists must have?
6. What other general skills should a psychiatrist have?

h. **Write a paragraph in which you summarize your research and discussion.**

9. RESEARCH

a. **Go online and find information to answer the questions below.**

1. Find at least two more jobs within mental health care.
2. What are the formal qualifications necessary to practice them?
3. What is the knowledge required to perform these jobs?
4. What are the personal skills necessary to do these jobs?
5. What are the general skills necessary for the jobs?

b. **Share your findings in groups.**

10. ESSAY WRITING

Use all your previous notes and write an essay in which you discuss mental healthcare jobs and skills. You can follow the guiding instructions provided below. Remember to give your essay a title.

ONE	Write an introduction in which you point out the importance of mental healthcare jobs, and introduce one job you believe is the most significant for you or in general.
TWO	Write a paragraph in which you discuss the *qualifications and knowledge* necessary to perform this job. Give examples, explanations, and details.
THREE	Write a paragraph in which you discuss the *personal skills* necessary to perform this job. Give examples, explanations, and details.
FOUR	Write a paragraph in which you discuss the *general skills* necessary to perform this job. Give examples, explanations, and details.
FIVE	Write a conclusion in which you discuss how important this job and skills are for the social life.

CHILDCARE

11. RESEARCH

    a. Go online and find information which will help you answer the questions below.

1. What is childcare?
2. What is childcare assistance?
3. Who are childcare professionals?
4. What are childcare benefits?
5. What are the differences between communal and private kindergartens?
6. What is the difference between an au-pair and a babysitter?
7. Do all countries have free childcare services?

    b. In groups, discuss the questions above. Take notes during your discussion.

    c. Write a paragraph in which you summarize your research and discussion.

12. WHAT DOES A KINDERGARTEN TEACHER DO?

    a. In groups, discuss the questions below. Go online to find out more when necessary. Take notes during your discussion.

1. What are the required qualifications to become a kindergarten teacher in your country?
2. What is the knowledge required to work as a kindergarten teacher?

3. What are the personal skills a kindergarten teacher should have? Make a list.
4. What are the general skills a kindergarten teacher should have? Make a list.

b. Write a paragraph in which you summarize your discussion.

c. In groups, describe a kindergarten teacher's typical day. In your description, include the words suggested below.

Arrival activities	Prepare the classroom
Parent meetings	Read aloud
Team meetings	Deliver lunch order to cafeteria
Rest time	Monitor children's learning
Play time	Debrief, plan, and prepare
Outdoors activities	Supervise out-of-doors activities
Preschool instruction	Write up observations on each child
Daily reports	Write in learners' journals

d. Write a paragraph in which you summarize your discussion.

e. In groups, discuss the questions below. Explain your views and offer examples.

1. Should a kindergarten teacher be more diligent or more creative?
2. Are you fit to work as a kindergarten teacher if you are not curious?
3. Are you apt to work as a kindergarten teacher if you are not patient?
4. Do you need to be passionate when you work as a kindergarten teacher?
5. How important is discipline for a kindergarten teacher?
6. What other personal skills should a kindergarten teacher have?

f. Write a paragraph in which you summarize your discussion.

g. **In groups, discuss the questions below. Explain your views and offer examples.**

1. Is flexibility a more significant skill than responsibility for a kindergarten teacher?
2. How important is emotional intelligence for a kindergarten teacher?
3. How important are observation skills for a kindergarten teacher?
4. Are strong communication skills fundamental for kindergarten teachers?
5. Is self-motivation crucial for the kindergarten teaching job?
6. What other general skills should a kindergarten teacher have?

h. **Write a paragraph in which you summarize your discussion.**

13. WHAT DOES A CHILD PSYCHOLOGIST DO?

a. **In groups, discuss the questions below. Go online to find out more when necessary. Take notes during your discussion.**

1. What are the required qualifications to become a child psychologist in your country?
2. What is the knowledge required to work as a child psychologist?
3. What are the personal skills a child psychologist should have? Make a list.
4. What are the general skills a child psychologist should have? Make a list.

b. **Write a paragraph in which you summarize your discussion.**

c. **In groups, describe a child psychologist's typical day. In your description, include the words suggested below.**

Family therapy sessions	Testify in court
Parent meetings	Make assessments
Group workshops	Diagnose emotional issues
Children who suffered trauma	Talk to children one-on-one
	Recommend routines and activities
Systematic observation	Collaborate with parents and schools
Child development	Collaborate with other health professionals
Abnormal child behavior	
	Provide children with support and understanding
Psychological issues	

d. **Write a paragraph in which you summarize your discussion.**

e. **In groups, discuss the questions below. Explain your views and offer examples.**

1. How does a child psychologist deal with emotional and behavioral issues?
2. Are you fit to work as a child psychologist if you are not curious?
3. Are you apt to work as a child psychologist if you are not patient?
4. Must you be passionate when you work as a child psychologist?
5. How important is perseverance for practicing child psychology?
6. What other personal skills should a child psychologist have?

f. **Write a paragraph in which you summarize your discussion.**

g. In groups, discuss the questions below. Explain your views and offer examples.

1. Is flexibility a more significant skill than responsibility for a child psychologist?
2. How important is emotional intelligence for a child psychologist?
3. How important are observation skills for child psychologists?
4. Are critical thinking skills fundamental for child psychologists?
5. Is self-motivation crucial for the job of a child psychologist?
6. What other general skills should a child psychologist have?

h. Write a paragraph in which you summarize your discussion.

14. RESEARCH

a. Go online and find information to answer the questions below.

1. Find at least two more jobs within childcare.
2. What are the formal qualifications necessary to practice them?
3. What is the knowledge required to perform these jobs?
4. What are the personal skills necessary to do these jobs?
5. What are the general skills necessary for the jobs?

b. Share your findings in groups.

15. ESSAY WRITING

Use all your previous notes and write an essay in which you discuss childcare jobs and skills. You can follow the guiding instructions provided below. Remember to give your essay a title.

ONE	Write an introduction in which you point out the importance of childcare jobs, and introduce one job you believe is the most significant for you or in general.
TWO	Write a paragraph in which you discuss the *qualifications and knowledge* necessary to perform this job. Give examples, explanations, and details.
THREE	Write a paragraph in which you discuss the *personal skills* necessary to perform this job. Give examples, explanations, and details.
FOUR	Write a paragraph in which you discuss the *general skills* necessary to perform this job. Give examples, explanations, and details.
FIVE	Write a conclusion in which you discuss how important this job and skills are for the social life.

EDUCATION

16. RESEARCH

    a. Go online and find information which will help you answer the questions below.

1. What is education?
2. What is formal and non-formal education?
3. What is vocational education?
4. What is university-preparatory education?
5. What is higher education?
6. Who provides education in a country?
7. Should all countries provide free higher education?

    b. In groups, discuss the questions above. Take notes during your discussion.

    c. Write a paragraph in which you summarize your research and discussion.

17. WHAT DOES A PRIMARY SCHOOL TEACHER DO?

    a. In groups, discuss the questions below. Go online to find out more when necessary. Take notes during your discussion.

1. What are the required qualifications to become a primary school teacher in your country?
2. What is the knowledge required to work as a primary school teacher?

3. What are the personal skills a primary school teacher should have? Make a list.
4. What are the general skills a primary school teacher should have? Make a list.

b. Write a paragraph in which you summarize your discussion.

c. In groups, describe a primary school teacher's typical day. In your description, include the words suggested below.

National curriculum	Track pupils' progress
Parent meetings	Mark books
Reading, writing, and speaking activities	Plan school trips
	Teach interesting sessions
Spelling practice	Monitor curricular activities and events
Professional development	Collaborate with parents and school leadership
Emotional resilience	
Behavior policy	Prepare resources and sort out lesson plans
Learning environment	Encourage pupils to use their skills and develop new ones
Photocopying	
	Handle ill-disciplined behavior

d. Write a paragraph in which you summarize your discussion.

e. In groups, discuss the questions below. Explain your views and offer examples.

1. Should a primary school teacher be more disciplined or more creative?
2. Are you fit to work as a primary school teacher if you are not curious?
3. Are you suitable for working as a primary school teacher if you are not confident?
4. Do you need to be patient when you work as a primary school teacher?
5. How important is passion for a primary school teacher?

6. What other personal skills should a primary school teacher have?

f. Write a paragraph in which you summarize your discussion.

g. In groups, discuss the questions below. Explain your views and offer examples.

1. Is observation a more significant skill than responsibility for a primary school teacher?
2. How important are listening skills versus speaking skills for a primary school teacher?
3. How important are cooperation skills for a primary school teacher?
4. Are strong communication skills fundamental for primary school teachers?
5. Is self-motivation crucial for the primary school teaching job?
6. What other general skills should a primary school teacher have?

h. Write a paragraph in which you summarize your discussion.

18. WHAT DOES AN ADULT EDUCATION TEACHER DO?

a. In groups, discuss the questions below. Go online to find out more when necessary. Take notes during your discussion.

1. What are the required qualifications to become an adult education teacher in your country?
2. What is the knowledge required to work as an adult education teacher?
3. What are the personal skills an adult education teacher should have? Make a list.
4. What are the general skills an adult education teacher should have? Make a list.

b. **Write a paragraph in which you summarize your discussion.**

c. **In groups, describe an adult education teacher's typical day. In your description, include the words suggested below.**

National curriculum	Track pupils' progress
Reading, writing, and speaking activities	Teach interesting sessions
	Monitor curricular activities and events
Professional development	Collaborate with school leadership
Emotional resilience	Prepare resources and sort out lesson plans
Behavior policy	Encourage students to use their skills and develop new ones
Learning environment	
Photocopying	

d. **Write a paragraph in which you summarize your discussion.**

e. **In groups, discuss the questions below. Explain your views and offer examples.**

1. Should an adult education teacher be more perseverant or more flexible?
2. Are you fit to work as an adult education teacher if you are not curious?
3. Are you suitable for working as an adult education teacher if you are not courageous?
4. Do you need to be ambitious when you work as an adult education teacher?
5. Can an adult education teacher be competent without being passionate?
6. What other personal skills should an adult education teacher have?

f. **Write a paragraph in which you summarize your discussion.**

g. **In groups, discuss the questions below. Explain your views and offer examples.**

1. Is observation a more significant skill than responsibility for an adult education teacher?
2. How important are listening skills versus speaking skills for an adult education teacher?
3. How important are conflict management skills for an adult education teacher?
4. Are strong communication skills fundamental for adult education teachers?
5. Is passion crucial for the adult education teaching job?
6. What other general skills should an adult education teacher have?

h. **Write a paragraph in which you summarize your discussion.**

19. RESEARCH

a. **Go online and find information to answer the questions below.**

1. Find at least two more jobs within education.
2. What are the formal qualifications necessary to practice them?
3. What is the knowledge required to perform these jobs?
4. What are the personal skills necessary to do these jobs?
5. What are the general skills necessary for the jobs?

b. **Share your findings in groups.**

20. ESSAY WRITING

Use all your previous notes and write an essay in which you discuss education jobs and skills. You can follow the guiding instructions provided below. Remember to give your essay a title.

ONE	Write an introduction in which you point out the importance of education jobs, and introduce one job you believe is the most significant for you or in general.
TWO	Write a paragraph in which you discuss the *qualifications and knowledge* necessary to perform this job. Give examples, explanations, and details.
THREE	Write a paragraph in which you discuss the *personal skills* necessary to perform this job. Give examples, explanations, and details.
FOUR	Write a paragraph in which you discuss the *general skills* necessary to perform this job. Give examples, explanations, and details.
FIVE	Write a conclusion in which you discuss how important this job and skills are for the social life.

ENGINEERING

21. RESEARCH

a. **Go online and find information which will help you answer the questions below.**

1. What is engineering?
2. What is civil engineering?
3. What is computer engineering?
4. What is environmental engineering?
5. What is biomedical engineering?
6. What is industrial/manufacturing engineering?
7. What is the importance of engineering for human progress?

b. **In groups, discuss the questions above. Take notes during your discussion.**

c. **Write a paragraph in which you summarize your research and discussion.**

22. WHAT DOES A CIVIL ENGINEER DO?

a. **In groups, discuss the questions below. Go online to find out more when necessary. Take notes during your discussion.**

1. What are the required qualifications to become a civil engineer in your country?
2. What is the knowledge required to work as a civil engineer?

3. What are the personal skills all civil engineers should have? Make a list.
4. What are the general skills all civil engineers should have? Make a list.

b. Write a paragraph in which you summarize your discussion.

c. In groups, describe a civil engineer's typical day. In your description, include the words suggested below.

Creation of a set of plans	Design constructions
Public hearings	Design plans for bridges
Applicable laws and regulations	Design parking lots
Project management	Design water and sewage systems
On-site client calls	Orchestrate airports and railroads
Face-to-face interaction	Maintain structures and facilities
Cost-effective projects	Plan irrigation projects
Survey reports	Study government regulations

d. Write a paragraph in which you summarize your discussion.

e. In groups, discuss the questions below. Explain your views and offer examples.

1. How important is patience versus curiosity in civil engineering?
2. Are you fit to work as a civil engineer if you are not detail oriented?
3. How important are creative skills for a civil engineer?
4. Should a civil engineer be more perseverant or more disciplined?
5. Is confidence a necessary skill for a civil engineer?
6. What other personal skills should all civil engineers have?

f. Write a paragraph in which you summarize your discussion.

g. **In groups, discuss the questions below. Explain your views and offer examples.**

1. Is observation a more significant skill than responsibility for a civil engineer?
2. How important are writing skills versus reading skills for a civil engineer?
3. How important are digital skills for a civil engineer?
4. Is critical thinking a fundamental skill for a civil engineer?
5. Should a civil engineer be a better problem solver or a better communicator?
6. What other general skills should civil engineers have?

h. **Write a paragraph in which you summarize your discussion.**

23. WHAT DOES AN ELECTRICAL ENGINEER DO?

a. **In groups, discuss the questions below. Go online to find out more when necessary. Take notes during your discussion.**

1. What are the required qualifications to become an electrical engineer in your country?
2. What is the knowledge required to work as an electrical engineer?
3. What are the personal skills all electrical engineers should have? Make a list.
4. What are the general skills all electrical engineers should have? Make a list.

b. **Write a paragraph in which you summarize your discussion.**

c. In groups, describe a civil engineer's typical day. In your description, include the words suggested below.

Application of electrical circuits	Confer with designers and architects
Architecture team leader	Discuss with interior and graphic design departments
First draft	Draw up representations and plans
Project proposal	Pre-research and brainstorm
Tight deadline	Use software to do calculations
3D cameras	Implement and test a project
Range detector	Troubleshoot when the scheme isn't working
Operating system	Prepare technical drawings of electrical systems

d. Write a paragraph in which you summarize your discussion.

e. In groups, discuss the questions below. Explain your views and offer examples.

1. How important is confidence in electrical engineering?
2. Are you fit to work as an electrical engineer if you are not patient?
3. How important are competition skills for an electrical engineer?
4. Should an electrical engineer be more confident or more disciplined?
5. Is passion a necessary skill for electrical engineers?
6. What other personal skills should electrical engineers have?

f. Write a paragraph in which you summarize your discussion.

g. In groups, discuss the questions below. Explain your views and offer examples.

1. How important are ethical reasoning skills for an electrical engineer?
2. How important are communication versus cooperation skills for an electrical engineer?
3. How important are digital skills for an electrical engineer?
4. Is conflict management a fundamental skill for an electrical engineer?
5. Should an electrical engineer be a better critical thinker or a better listener?
6. What other general skills should electrical engineers have?

h. Write a paragraph in which you summarize your discussion.

24. RESEARCH

a. Go online and find information to answer the questions below.

1. Find at least two more jobs within engineering.
2. What are the formal qualifications necessary to practice them?
3. What is the knowledge required to perform these jobs?
4. What are the personal skills necessary to do these jobs?
5. What are the general skills necessary for the jobs?

b. Share your findings in groups.

25. ESSAY WRITING

Use all your previous notes and write an essay in which you discuss engineering jobs and skills. You can follow the guiding instructions provided below. Remember to give your essay a title.

ONE	Write an introduction in which you point out the importance of engineering jobs, and introduce one job you believe is the most significant for you or in general.
TWO	Write a paragraph in which you discuss the *qualifications and knowledge* necessary to perform this job. Give examples, explanations, and details.
THREE	Write a paragraph in which you discuss the *personal skills* necessary to perform this job. Give examples, explanations, and details.
FOUR	Write a paragraph in which you discuss the *general skills* necessary to perform this job. Give examples, explanations, and details.
FIVE	Write a conclusion in which you discuss how important this job and skills are for the social life.

FOOD SERVICE

26. RESEARCH

a. **Go online and find information which will help you answer the questions below.**

1. What is food service?
2. Who offers food services?
3. What is the difference between catering and counter service?
4. What is the difference between buffet and table service?
5. What is the difference between a fast food and a fine dining restaurant?
6. What does a food service worker do?
7. What is an institutional food service management?

b. **In groups, discuss the questions above. Take notes during your discussion.**

c. **Write a paragraph in which you summarize your research and discussion.**

27. WHAT DOES A CHEF DO?

a. **In groups, discuss the questions below. Go online to find out more when necessary. Take notes during your discussion.**

1. What are the required qualifications to become a chef in your country?
2. What is the knowledge required to work as a chef?
3. What are the personal skills all chefs should have? Make a list.

4. What are the general skills all chefs should have? Make a list.

b. Write a paragraph in which you summarize your discussion.

c. In groups, describe a chef's typical day. In your description, include the words suggested below.

Culinary art	Take inventory of food and beverages
Part-time personnel manager	Make additions or changes to the menu
Long hours and stressful conditions	Chop and slice vegetables, and make sauces
Creative control	Supervise and coordinate staff preparation and performance
Love of food	Plan and review the menu
Early riser	Be on your feet for long stretches of time
Multiple recipes and ingredients	Be highly adaptable and creative
Service and rush	Create recipes and craft new dishes
Plating and firing courses	

d. Write a paragraph in which you summarize your discussion.

e. In groups, discuss the questions below. Explain your views and offer examples.

1. How important is passion on the job of a chef?
2. Are you fit to work as a chef if you are not disciplined?
3. How important are competitive skills for a chef?
4. Should a chef be more ambitious or more proactive?
5. Is curiosity a necessary skill for a chef?
6. What other personal skills should all chefs have?

f. **Write a paragraph in which you summarize your discussion.**

g. **In groups, discuss the questions below. Explain your views and offer examples.**

1. Is observation a more significant skill than responsibility for a chef?
2. How important are listening skills versus speaking skills for a chef?
3. How important is self-motivation for a chef?
4. Is conflict management a fundamental skill for a chef?
5. Should a chef be a better problem solver or a better communicator?
6. What other general skills should chefs have?

h. **Write a paragraph in which you summarize your discussion.**

28. WHAT DOES A RESTAURANT MANAGER DO?

a. **In groups, discuss the questions below. Go online to find out more when necessary. Take notes during your discussion.**

1. What are the required qualifications to become a restaurant manager in your country?
2. What is the knowledge required to work as a restaurant manager?
3. What are the personal skills all restaurant managers should have? Make a list.
4. What are the general skills all restaurant managers should have? Make a list.

b. **Write a paragraph in which you summarize your discussion.**

c. **In groups, describe a restaurant manager's typical day. In your description, include the words suggested below.**

Culinary fares	Run a restaurant
Supervisory skills	Coordinate employees
Fast-paced environment	Evaluate employees regularly
Paperwork and communication	Order food and supplies
Employee scheduling	Pay suppliers
Business performance responsibility	Oversee food deliveries
	Prepare payrolls and taxes
Sales and profitability	Prepare weekly reports
Budgets and menus	Organize marketing activities
Customer complaints	Schedule shifts
Staff recruitment and training	

d. **Write a paragraph in which you summarize your discussion.**

e. **In groups, discuss the questions below. Explain your views and offer examples.**

1. How important is flexibility for the job of a restaurant manager?
2. Are you fit to work as a restaurant manager if you are not disciplined?
3. How important is ambition for a restaurant manager?
4. Should a restaurant manager be more curious or more proactive?
5. Is confidence a necessary skill for a restaurant manager?
6. What other personal skills should restaurant managers have?

f. **Write a paragraph in which you summarize your discussion.**

g. **In groups, discuss the questions below. Explain your views and offer examples.**

1. Is responsibility a more significant skill than observation for a restaurant manager?
2. How important are listening skills versus speaking skills for a restaurant manager?
3. How important is emotional intelligence for a restaurant manager?
4. Is conflict management a fundamental skill for a restaurant manager?
5. Should a restaurant manager be a better problem solver or a better ethical reasoner?
6. What other general skills should restaurant managers have?

h. **Write a paragraph in which you summarize your discussion.**

29. RESEARCH

a. **Go online and find information to answer the questions below.**

1. Find at least two more jobs within food service.
2. What are the formal qualifications necessary to practice them?
3. What is the knowledge required to perform these jobs?
4. What are the personal skills necessary to do these jobs?
5. What are the general skills necessary for the jobs?

b. **Share your findings in groups.**

30. ESSAY WRITING

Use all your previous notes and write an essay in which you discuss food service jobs and skills. You can follow the guiding instructions provided below. Remember to give your essay a title.

ONE	Write an introduction in which you point out the importance of food service jobs, and introduce one job you believe is the most significant for you or in general.
TWO	Write a paragraph in which you discuss the *qualifications and knowledge* necessary to perform this job. Give examples, explanations, and details.
THREE	Write a paragraph in which you discuss the *personal skills* necessary to perform this job. Give examples, explanations, and details.
FOUR	Write a paragraph in which you discuss the *general skills* necessary to perform this job. Give examples, explanations, and details.
FIVE	Write a conclusion in which you discuss how important this job and skills are for the social life.

TRADESMANSHIP

31. RESEARCH

a. **Go online and find information which will help you answer the questions below.**

1. What is a trade?
2. What are skilled trades?
3. What are semiskilled trades?
4. What is a vocational training program?
5. What are supply and demand?
6. What are some high paying skilled trades?
7. What are blue-color and white-color jobs?

b. **In groups, discuss the questions above. Take notes during your discussion.**

c. **Write a paragraph in which you summarize your research and discussion.**

32. WHAT DOES AN ELECTRICIAN DO?

a. **In groups, discuss the questions below. Go online to find out more when necessary. Take notes during your discussion.**

1. What are the required qualifications to become an electrician in your country?
2. What is the knowledge required to work as an electrician?
3. What are the personal skills an electrician should have? Make a list.

4. What are the general skills an electrician should have? Make a list.

b. **Write a paragraph in which you summarize your discussion.**

c. **In groups, describe an electrician's typical day. In your description, include the words suggested below.**

Challenging electrical problems	Work during off hours
Standard 9 to 5 shift	Be on-call for electricity emergencies
Wire and voltage problems	
Solar panels	Get the power back
An independent contractor	Install and repair wiring
Damaged circuit breakers	Review the blueprints of a project
Regular check-up and maintenance	Know regional and national building codes
Drills, hacksaws and wire strippers	Delegate tasks
	Test wires and sockets

d. **Write a paragraph in which you summarize your discussion.**

e. **In groups, discuss the questions below. Explain your views and offer examples.**

1. Should an electrician be more confident or more diligent?
2. Is perseverance a fundamental skill for an electrician?
3. Are you fit to work as an electrician if you are not detail oriented?
4. Can an electrician with no confidence do his job properly?
5. Do you need to be courageous to work as an electrician?
6. What other personal skills should electricians have?

f. **Write a paragraph in which you summarize your discussion.**

g. **In groups, discuss the questions below. Explain your views and offer examples.**

1. Is observation a more significant skill than responsibility for an electrician?
2. Is reading a more important skill than listening for an electrician?
3. Should an electrician be better at thinking critically or solving problems?
4. Is digital competence a crucial skill for an electrician?
5. Do electricians need strong cooperation skills?
6. What other general skills should electricians have?

h. **Write a paragraph in which you summarize your discussion.**

33. WHAT DOES A CARPENTER DO?

a. **In groups, discuss the questions below. Go online to find out more when necessary. Take notes during your discussion.**

1. What are the required qualifications to become a carpenter in your country?
2. What is the knowledge required to work as a carpenter?
3. What are the personal skills a carpenter should possess? Make a list.
4. What are the general skills a carpenter should possess? Make a list.

b. **Write a paragraph in which you summarize your discussion.**

c. **In groups, describe a carpenter's typical day. In your description, include the words suggested below.**

Carpentry crew	Study sketches and building plans
Hand tools and machines	
Windows, frames, hardware, and floorings	Mark cutting lines on materials
	Cut materials to specific measurements
Ceilings and floors	
Safety shoes, gloves, and glasses	Install fixtures and structures
Strenuous manual labor	Follow safety rules
Furniture repairer or restorer	Prepare project layouts
Restoration techniques	Build or repair wooden fixtures
	Assemble structures

d. **Write a paragraph in which you summarize your discussion.**

e. **In groups, discuss the questions below. Explain your views and offer examples.**

1. Should carpenters be more sociable or more curious?
2. If you are not courageous, are you fit to be a carpenter?
3. Is confidence a skill carpenters need?
4. Should a carpenter be more detail oriented or more disciplined?
5. Can a carpenter who is not passionate about his job be competent?
6. What other personal skills should carpenters have?

f. **Write a paragraph in which you summarize your discussion.**

g. **In groups, discuss the questions below. Explain your views and offer examples.**

1. Are critical thinking skills important to do the job of a carpenter?
2. Should a carpenter listen more than speak, and write more than read?
3. As a carpenter, is it more important to be observant or to be communicative?
4. How important is responsibility for the work of a carpenter?
5. If you are not a proficient problem solver, are you fit for practicing carpentry?
6. What other general skills should carpenters possess?

h. **Write a paragraph in which you summarize your discussion.**

34. RESEARCH

a. **Go online and find information to answer the questions below.**

1. Find at least two more jobs within tradesmanship.
2. What are the formal qualifications necessary to practice them?
3. What is the knowledge required to perform these jobs?
4. What are the personal skills necessary to do these jobs?
5. What are the general skills necessary for the jobs?

b. **Share your findings in groups.**

35. ESSAY WRITING

Use all previous notes and write an essay in which you discuss tradesmanship jobs and skills. You can follow the guiding instructions provided below. Remember to give your essay a title.

ONE	Write an introduction in which you point out the importance of tradesmanship jobs, and introduce one job you believe is the most significant for you or in general.
TWO	Write a paragraph in which you discuss the *qualifications and knowledge* necessary to perform this job. Give examples, explanations, and details.
THREE	Write a paragraph in which you discuss the *personal skills* necessary to perform this job. Give examples, explanations, and details.
FOUR	Write a paragraph in which you discuss the *general skills* necessary to perform this job. Give examples, explanations, and details.
FIVE	Write a conclusion in which you discuss how important this job and skills are for the social life.

MEDIA AND JOURNALISM

36. RESEARCH

a. **Go online and find information which will help you answer the questions below.**

1. What is journalism?
2. What are communication technologies?
3. What is the difference between multimedia and digital journalism?
4. What are social media?
5. What is advocacy journalism?
6. What is non-profit journalism?
7. What is journalism ethics?

b. **In groups, discuss the questions above. Take notes during your discussion.**

c. **Write a paragraph in which you summarize your research and discussion.**

37. WHAT DOES A JOURNALIST DO?

a. **In groups, discuss the questions below. Go online to find out more when necessary. Take notes during your discussion.**

1. What are the required qualifications to become a journalist in your country?
2. What is the knowledge required to work as a journalist?
3. What are the personal skills a journalist should have? Make a list.

4. What are the general skills a journalist should have? Make a list.

b. Write a paragraph in which you summarize your discussion.

c. In groups, describe a journalist's typical day. In your description, include the words suggested below.

Online marketplace	Engage with the audience
Home-grown website	Compete with social media
Traditional publications	Hold interviews
Reporting and analysis	Confer with editors and feature
In-depth conversation with editors	writers
	Communicate and network
Current stories and events	Generate ideas and find stories
Though-provoking pieces	Be interested in current affairs and politics
Office-based work	
	Throw yourself into the fire

d. Write a paragraph in which you summarize your discussion.

e. In groups, discuss the questions below. Explain your views and offer examples.

1. Should a journalist be more courageous or more passionate?
2. Is empathy a fundamental skill for a journalist?
3. Are you fit to work as a journalist if you are not curious?
4. Can a journalist with no social skills do his/her job properly?
5. Do you need to be ambitious to work as a journalist?
6. What other personal skills should journalists have?

f. Write a paragraph in which you summarize your discussion.

MEDIA AND JOURNALISM

g. In groups, discuss the questions below. Explain your views and offer examples.

1. Is observation a more significant skill than responsibility for a journalist?
2. Is writing a more important skill than listening for a journalist?
3. Should a journalist be better at thinking critically or solving problems?
4. Is emotional intelligence a crucial skill for a journalist?
5. Do journalists need strong ethical reasoning skills?
6. What other general skills should journalists have?

h. Write a paragraph in which you summarize your discussion.

38. WHAT DOES A MULTIMEDIA WRITER DO?

a. In groups, discuss the questions below. Go online to find out more when necessary. Take notes during your discussion.

1. What are the required qualifications to become a multimedia writer?
2. What is the knowledge required to work as a multimedia writer?
3. What are the personal skills a multimedia writer should have? Make a list.
4. What are the general skills a multimedia writer should have? Make a list.

b. Write a paragraph in which you summarize your discussion.

c. **In groups, describe a multimedia writer's typical day. In your description, include the words suggested below.**

Creativity and technology	Create texts for ad campaigns
Problem-solving	Produce content and write scripts
Well-developed portfolio	Conduct research
Graphic design	Review story ideas
Video and photo editing programs	Check facts and analyze data
	Strategize topic ideas
Video games system	Write content for magazines newsletters
Educational tools	
Production process	Create content for radio and television broadcasts

d. **Write a paragraph in which you summarize your discussion.**

e. **In groups, discuss the questions below. Explain your views and offer examples.**

1. Should a multimedia writer be more curious or more creative?
2. Is confidence a fundamental skill for a multimedia writer?
3. Are you fit to work as a multimedia writer if you are not flexible?
4. Can a multimedia writer with no proactive skills do his/her job properly?
5. Do you need to be competitive to work as a multimedia writer?
6. What other personal skills should multimedia writers have?

f. **Write a paragraph in which you summarize your discussion.**

g. In groups, discuss the questions below. Explain your views and offer examples.

1. Is observation a more significant skill than self-motivation for a multimedia writer?
2. Is listening a more important skill than speaking for a multimedia writer?
3. Should a multimedia writer be better at critical thinking or conflict management?
4. Is cooperation more important than communication for a multimedia writer?
5. Do multimedia writers need strong ethical reasoning skills?
6. What other general skills should multimedia writers have?

h. Write a paragraph in which you summarize your discussion.

39. RESEARCH

a. Go online and find information to answer the questions below.

1. Find at least two more jobs within media and journalism.
2. What are the formal qualifications necessary to practice them?
3. What is the knowledge required to perform these jobs?
4. What are the personal skills necessary to do these jobs?
5. What are the general skills necessary for the jobs?

b. Share your findings in groups.

40. ESSAY WRITING

Use all your previous notes and write an essay in which you discuss media and journalism jobs and skills. You can follow the guiding instructions provided below. Remember to give your essay a title.

ONE	Write an introduction in which you point out the importance of media and journalism jobs, and introduce one job you believe is the most significant for you or in general.
TWO	Write a paragraph in which you discuss the *qualifications and knowledge* necessary to perform this job. Give examples, explanations, and details.
THREE	Write a paragraph in which you discuss the *personal skills* necessary to perform this job. Give examples, explanations, and details.
FOUR	Write a paragraph in which you discuss the *general skills* necessary to perform this job. Give examples, explanations, and details.
FIVE	Write a conclusion in which you discuss how important this job and skills are for the social life.

CHAPTER 4

SKILLS FOR THE FUTURE

> *This chapter includes a few skills which will be paramount in the future. Dealing with information, choosing reliable sources, and sorting out relevance from irrelevance is going to be key for career success in the future. Information will only constitute the tools necessary to solve very complex problems.*

DEALING WITH AMBIGUITY

1. SPEAKING

Discuss in groups. Share with the class.

1. What makes a situation or experience unsettling or anxiety-provoking?
2. Why do we fear what seems uncertain and unknowable?
3. How do you handle unease?
4. How should you handle unease?

2. VOCABULARY

a. **Consult a dictionary and do research online to define the terms below.**

INTUITIVE JUDGMENT	
INTERPRETATIVE ABILITY	
A STATE OF LIMBO	
MENTAL PARALYSIS	
IMPACT ANTICIPATION	
CRYSTAL-CLEAR THINKING	
ANXIETY MANAGEMENT	
BEHAVIORAL COMPETENCE	

b. Underline one phrase which does not belong in each set.

1. Rely on your intuition / deal successfully with pressure / focused on a pre-planned goal
2. Bounce back from frustration / worry about the outcome of your decision / use your imagination
3. Overanalyze before making a decision / focus on the present moment / have confidence in your own judgment

c. Find synonyms for the words below.

1. Debatable	_____
2. Misleading	_____
3. Puzzling	_____
4. Doubtful	_____
5. Equivocal	_____

d. Find antonyms for the words below.

1. Evident	_____
2. Beyond doubt	_____
3. Unmistakable	_____
4. Irrefutable	_____
5. Conclusive	_____

3. SPEAKING AND WRITING

a. Discuss in groups.

1. Describe an ambiguous answer.
2. Describe an ambiguous assignment.
3. Describe an ambiguous person.
4. Describe a vague feeling.
5. Describe an uncertain situation.

b. Summarize your discussion in a paragraph or two.

c. **Write an example to illustrate each statement below. Share them in groups.**

1. It is disadvantageous to want things black or white all the time.
   Example: _____
2. Sometimes, you have to make a judgment call based on vague communication.
   Example: _____
3. Today's typical workplace blurs the lines between responsibility and leadership.
   Example: _____
4. Every employee should deal with complex situations with no familiar cues or solutions.
   Example: _____
5. Working life requires the ability to be comfortable with risk and uncertainty.
   Example: _____

d. **Complete the sentences below with one of the alternatives in the box.**

unpredictable ambivalence resilience ambiguity explicitness uncertainty ambiguity vague uncertain imagination

1. _____ is especially hard for people who are not good at prioritizing.
2. Sometimes, _____ can be a sign of poor relation between language and thought.
3. Good communication always relies on _____ .
4. _____ can be very unsettling, but it also urges us to act in novel ways.
5. The world rewards people who remain cool in very _____ or complex situations.
6. It is true that sometimes people use _____ language to express disapproval.
7. However, self-control and _____ change setbacks into useful experiences.

8. One way to deal with _____ is by engaging in thought experiments.
9. Thought experiments rely on the use of _____ to explore the nature of things.
10. They help us evaluate and predict potential outcomes in _____ situations.

e. Pick one sentence from the previous task and explain it with details and examples in a paragraph.

f. Agree or disagree with the statements below. Discuss your reasons in groups.

1. When you let fear enter an ambiguous situation, you let rationality out.
2. All situations in life are somewhat ambiguous, because we rarely have access to all relevant information.
3. When you think about it, every word we say is somewhat ambiguous.
4. Ambiguous situations are especially overwhelming when you get stuck on a single solution or outcome.

4. ESSAY WRITING

Write an essay in which you comment on the statement below. Remember to offer reasons and examples. You might want to do some research on terms like *intuition, strategic thinking,* **and** *thought experiments.*

A big part of life consists of uncertainties, but knowing this does not make ambiguity any less unsettling. However, learning how to deal with ambiguity is learning how to deal with life's unpredictability.

ONE	Write an introduction in which you present ambiguity as an important part of life, and why it is an important skill.
TWO	Write a paragraph in which you discuss how ambiguous situations are pervasive in all fields of life. Give examples, explanations, and details.
THREE	Write a paragraph in which you discuss *one way* to deal with ambiguity. Give examples, explanations, and details.
FOUR	Write a paragraph in which you discuss *another way* to deal with ambiguity. Give examples, explanations, and details.
FIVE	Write a conclusion in which you discuss how important it is to deal with ambivalent aspects of life.

AVOIDING CONFIRMATION BIAS

5. SPEAKING

Discuss in groups. Share with the class.

1. How can you know that you understand something clearly?
2. How can you know when you hold false beliefs?
3. Can you always explain the reasons behind your beliefs?
4. Should you always be able to explain the reasons behind your beliefs?

6. VOCABULARY

a. Consult a dictionary and do research online to define the terms below.

COGNITIVE BIAS	
TRIBAL THINKING	
TUNNEL VISION	
INTELLECTUAL HUMILITY	
METACOGNITION	
SELF-SERVING BIAS	
MENTAL SHORTCUTS	
HALO EFFECT	

b. Underline one phrase which does not belong in each set.

1. Transcend raw emotions / overcome illogical thought / it warps your thoughts
2. Be deluded / courageous truth telling / superstitions and prejudices
3. It nourishes your convictions / it supports your existing beliefs / it challenges your opinions

c. Find synonyms for the words below.

1. Biased	_____
2. One-sided	_____
3. Discriminatory	_____
4. Prejudicial	_____
5. Distorted	_____

d. Find antonyms for the words below.

1. Subjective	_____
2. Unfair	_____
3. Partial	_____
4. Skewed	_____
5. Unjustified	_____

7. SPEAKING AND WRITING

a. Discuss in groups.

1. Describe a biased opinion.
2. Describe a biased result.
3. Describe a biased media coverage.
4. Describe biased information.
5. Describe a prejudicial attitude.

b. **Summarize your discussion in a paragraph or two.**

c. **Write an example to illustrate each statement below. Share in groups.**

1. It is dangerous to always look for information that confirms your biases.
   Example: _____
2. An intelligent person is interested in other points of view than one's own.
   Example: _____
3. One way to avoid confirmation bias is to consider alternatives.
   Example: _____
4. Focusing on information that confirms your beliefs can result in poor decisions.
   Example: _____
5. Working life requires the ability to reflect on situations and their multiple perspectives.
   Example: _____

d. **Complete the sentences below with one of the alternatives in the box.**

unsettling fallacies facts uncritically unprepared subtle limited confirmation embrace misconceptions

1. One of the of the most well-known cognitive biases is the _____ bias.
2. Confirmation bias consists in embracing _____ evidence that reinforces your view.
3. It is common for people today to avoid _____ which seem to threaten their standpoint.
4. Cognitive biases, however, are not easy to detect, as they are very _____ and pervasive.
5. It is tempting to _____ evidence which is agreeable with your own world view.
6. But this makes you incapable of accepting your own _____ .

7. This in return renders you _____ for a world in which critical thinking is vital.
8. One should always be able to transcend one's own _____ understanding.
9. Confirmation bias results from rejecting every evidence one finds _____ .
10. But by doing that, you surround yourself by a plethora of _____ and delusions.

e. Pick one sentence from the previous task and explain it with details and examples in a paragraph.

f. Agree or disagree with the statements below. Discuss your reasons in groups.

1. Everybody has beliefs, but believing in something does not make it true.
2. No matter how hard we may try, it is impossible to see an experience through multiple perspectives.
3. You cannot succeed in work and life if you are unable to give reasons for your opinions.
4. To be able to explain your behavior with good reasons is the skill of a reflective mind.

8. ESSAY WRITING

Write an essay in which you comment on the statement below. Remember to offer reasons and examples. You might want to do some research on terms like *natural selection, tribal thinking, identity politics, social cooperation* and *group mentality*.

Natural selection has saddled us with cognitive biases, and it is very hard to escape them. However, we can always fight our cognitive biases with intellectual humility.

ONE	Write an introduction in which you define the terms you will use and how they influence cognitive biases.
TWO	Write a paragraph in which you discuss how cognitive biases are so pervasive, and why we easily become prey for them. Give examples, explanations, and details.
THREE	Write a paragraph in which you discuss *one way* of how intellectual humility can help us escape cognitive biases. Give examples, explanations, and details.
FOUR	Write a paragraph in which you discuss *another way* of how intellectual humility can help us escape cognitive biases. Give examples, explanations, and details.
FIVE	Write a conclusion in which you discuss how important it is to avoid confirmation bias.

COGNITIVE FLEXIBILITY

9. SPEAKING

Discuss in groups. Share with the class.

1. Is it always easy to learn new things?
2. How do we deal with changes in our environment?
3. How does experience facilitate learning?
4. Would we succeed without the capacity for adaptation?

10. VOCABULARY

a. **Consult a dictionary and do research online to define the terms below.**

MENTAL PROCESS	
BEHAVIORAL RESPONSE	
ATTENTIONAL FLEXIBILITY	
COGNITIVE BLOCKADE	
DIVERGENT THINKING	
FALSE DIAGNOSIS	
KNOWLEDGE REORGANIZATION	
KNOWLEDGE TRANSFER	

b. Underline one phrase which does not belong in each set.

1. Perform a complex task / focus attention on the process / fail to interpret a new situation
2. Refuse to address the new task requirements / access the new situation / restructure knowledge
3. Perceive new environmental conditions / stick to knowledge from previous experience / plan a new sequence of actions

c. Find synonyms for the words below.

1. Perceive	_____
2. Adapt	_____
3. Reinterpret	_____
4. Respond	_____
5. Restructure	_____

d. Find antonyms for the words below.

1. Versatile	_____
2. Stretchable	_____
3. Resourceful	_____
4. Open to change	_____
5. Resilient	_____

11. SPEAKING AND WRITING

a. Discuss in groups.

1. Describe a cognitive experience.
2. Describe some cognitive goals.
3. Describe a situation demanding to adapt to new information.
4. Describe how a person adapts to new situations.

COGNITIVE FLEXIBILITY

b. Summarize your discussion in a paragraph or two.

c. Write an example to illustrate each statement below. Share in groups.

1. Most activities today require that we disengage from one task and respond to another.
   Example: _____
2. An effective person should be able to think about multiple ideas simultaneously.
   Example: _____
3. Many working situations demand that employees solve problems based on new information.
   Example: _____
4. Seeking out new experiences can be one way to increase your cognitive flexibility.
   Example: _____
5. You can build up cognitive flexibility by changing up your routine.
   Example: _____

d. Complete the sentences below with one of the alternatives in the box.

> backgrounds knowledge enhance contexts adaptable increase creative access limitless "right"

1. New experiences make us more _____ to different surroundings.
2. Every time we experience something new, we also _____ our memory and learning.
3. For example, travelling to different places gives us _____ to new ways of understanding.
4. When we engage in novel activities, such as learning a new language, we _____ our cognitive flexibility.
5. Cognitively flexible people tend to think in unconventional and _____ ways.
6. Cognitive flexibility also includes transferring _____ from one domain to another.

7. Applying known concepts to new _____ can have a great impact on our cognitive abilities.
8. Cognitive flexibility relies on thinking in terms of _____ possibilities.
9. Meeting new people with different _____ is a great way to challenge our cognitive elasticity.
10. One should always keep in mind that there is more than one _____ way to see things.

e. Pick one sentence from the previous task and explain it with details and examples in a paragraph.

f. Agree or disagree with the statements below. Discuss your reasons in groups.

1. You cannot improve yourself if you avoid challenging your own beliefs.
2. There is no use in learning anything you cannot transfer to real-world situations.
3. An intelligent person is aware that today's understanding of something can be altered tomorrow.
4. If you find something easy, you are not learning.

12. ESSAY WRITING

Write an essay in which you comment on the statement below. Remember to offer reasons and examples.

The future belongs to people who are always ready to learn new things and adjust to new situations.

ONE	Write an introduction in which you present cognitive flexibility as the skill of the future.
TWO	Write a paragraph in which you discuss *cognitive flexibility in the workplace*. Give examples, explanations, and details.
THREE	Write a paragraph in which you discuss *cognitive flexibility in all other fields of life*. Give examples, explanations, and details.
FOUR	Write a paragraph in which you discuss *different ways to enhance cognitive flexibility*. Give examples, explanations, and details.
FIVE	Write a conclusion in which you discuss how important cognitive flexibility is for a satisfying life.

DEEP FOCUS

13. SPEAKING

Discuss in groups. Share with the class.

1. Why is today's world described as full of distractions?
2. How do these distractions influence the way we work?
3. Can one be creative and productive without deep focus?
4. What are the ideal conditions for deep learning and work?

14. VOCABULARY

a. Consult a dictionary and do research online to define the terms below.

ATTENTION SPAN	
FRAGMENTED ATTENTION	
INTENTIONAL PRACTICE	
MIND WANDERING	
MENTAL PROCESS	
PEAK TIME	
INFORMATION OVERLOAD	
SHALLOW WORK	

b. Underline one phrase which does not belong in each set.

1. Remove distractions / focus on a single task / different notifications competing for your attention
2. Leave time to accomplish complex tasks / multitasking while working / keep a clean work environment
3. Switch permanently tasks / non-peak times of the day / explore alternative solutions

c. Find synonyms for the words below.

1. Performance	_____
2. Productivity	_____
3. Distraction	_____
4. Concentration	_____
5. Alertness	_____

d. Find antonyms for the words below.

1. Optimal	_____
2. Demanding	_____
3. Indispensable	_____
4. Shallow	_____
5. Intense	_____

15. SPEAKING AND WRITING

a. Discuss in groups.

1. Describe a working situation full of distractions.
2. Describe a distraction-free working environment.
3. Make a list of complex tasks which can be done only in a distraction-free setting.
4. Describe the ideal working environment for you. When do your cognitive powers peak?

b. **Summarize your discussion in a paragraph or two.**

c. **Write an example to illustrate each statement below. Share in groups.**

1. One cannot work on a demanding task without removing all distractions.
   Example: _____
2. Our digital environment makes it very hard to focus deeply on extended periods of time.
   Example: _____
3. Multitasking results quite often in misunderstandings and mistakes.
   Example: _____
4. Difficult tasks and learning happen only in distraction-free spaces.
   Example: _____
5. Deep focus is a matter of practice and we should train our mind like a muscle.
   Example: _____

d. **Complete the sentences below with one of the alternatives in the box.**

attention essential complete distractions carefully master downsides creativity concentration spaces

1. Multitasking has more _____ than benefits.
2. Deep focus helps us _____ complicated information.
3. Attention is a rare commodity and should be allotted _____ .
4. Unbroken _____ over long stretches of time is the only way to get real work done.
5. Notifications and _____ drain our energy and depletes our power of attention.
6. That is why it is _____ to turn off all distractions and commit our attention to one task.
7. Ideal conditions of work can make us feel sharper and _____ our work easier.

8. We should monitor our own _____ and manage effectively our attentional resources.
9. Quiet _____ make you slow down and at the same time speed up your thinking.
10. The greatest minds of history knew how invaluable attentional control is for_____ .

e. Pick one sentence from the previous task and explain it with details and examples in a paragraph.

f. Agree or disagree with the statements below. Discuss your reasons in groups.

1. Understanding your brain's limitations is crucial to thriving in the information age.
2. The mastery of new intellectual skills is unlikely to happen without deep concentration.
3. The internet has fragmented our thinking and working, and it is destructive.
4. There is nothing wrong with a fragmented way of life. In fact, the internet is a blessing for the curious mind. It is a treasure for those who are eager to learn continuously.

16. ESSAY WRITING

Write an essay in which you comment on the statement below. Remember to offer reasons and examples.

The future belongs to people who are capable of deep focus in a world full of distractions.

ONE	Write an introduction in which you present deep focus as the skill of the future.
TWO	Write a paragraph in which you discuss *deep focus in the workplace*. Give examples, explanations, and details.
THREE	Write a paragraph in which you discuss *deep focus in all other fields of life*. Give examples, explanations, and details.
FOUR	Write a paragraph in which you discuss *different ways to enhance concentration skills*. Give examples, explanations, and details.
FIVE	Write a conclusion in which you discuss how important deep focus is for a creative and meaningful life.

DIALECTICAL THINKING

17. SPEAKING

Discuss in groups. Share with the class.

1. What makes dialectical thinking a fundamental future skill?
2. What makes considering an issue from multiple perspectives important?
3. How can we deal with contradictory information?
4. Is it possible to consider an issue from several points of view simultaneously?

18. VOCABULARY

a. Consult a dictionary and do research online to define the terms below.

CAUSALITY	
ANALYSIS	
THESIS	
ANTITHESIS	
SYNTHESIS	
SOCRATIC DIALOGUE	
EXPERIENTIAL KNOWLEDGE	
POLARIZATION	

b. Underline one phrase which does not belong in each set.

1. Opposing sides / multiples perspectives / a driving force
2. Adopt an attitude of openness / a one-sidedly formed opinion / build awareness of one's own judgment
3. Remove feelings of self-righteousness / black and white thinking / learn to see life as a grey area

c. Find synonyms for the words below.

1. Engage	_____
2. Nurture	_____
3. Debate	_____
4. Foster	_____
5. Culminate	_____

d. Find antonyms for the words below.

1. Roadblock	_____
2. Collision	_____
3. Advocacy	_____
4. Adherence	_____
5. Multiplicity	_____

19. SPEAKING AND WRITING

a. Discuss in groups.

1. Give an example of a thesis, develop a contradictory antithesis, and finish with a synthesis.
2. Would we know what is right without knowing what is wrong?
3. What are the implications of never engaging in dialectical thinking?
4. What are the skills related to the willingness to permanently question your opinions?

b. **Summarize your discussion in a paragraph or two.**

c. **Write an example to illustrate each statement below. Share in groups.**

1. Critical thinking is vital for self-knowledge and exploration.
   Example: _____
2. Through critical thinking we realize our own limitations and biases.
   Example: _____
3. We acquire new ideas and ways of thinking through our interactions with other people.
   Example: _____
4. We join in dialectical thinking because we want to resolve conflicting viewpoints.
   Example: _____
5. A conflict can be resolved by synthesizing two divergent positions or logically favoring one.
   Example: _____

d. **Complete the sentences below with one of the alternatives in the box.**

review perspective strong comparing moral examination inquiry dilemmas opposing development

1. Human _____ occurs in interpersonal interactions and conflict resolutions.
2. Dialectical thinking helps us understand different concepts by _____ and contrasting them.
3. Dialectical thinking improves empathy skills by considering another's_____ .
4. Making moral judgments would be hard to achieve without a consideration of_____ opinions.
5. Engaging in moral _____ one get to become aware of one's fundamental values.

6. Humans should engage in a continuous _____ of their beliefs and the reasons behind them.
7. A critical _____ of opposing theories and arguments makes us equipped to live life well.
8. Moral _____ helps people become responsible beings.
9. Every intelligent person should be able to distinguish weak arguments from _____ ones.
10. Dialectical thinking can resolve physical and _____ conflicts between individuals and nations.

e. Pick one sentence from the previous task and explain it with details and examples in a paragraph.

f. Agree or disagree with the statements below. Discuss your reasons in groups.

1. Change is possible only through opposition and dissent.
2. There is no point in trying to see an issue from an opposing perspective if you are not open to change your own view.
3. Life becomes confusing if one never establishes one final opinion as the truth.
4. Sometimes, emotions are a better guide to the truth than logical thinking.

20. ESSAY WRITING

Write an essay in which you comment on the statement below. Remember to offer reasons and examples.

The future belongs to people who are capable of entertaining multiple perspectives and engage in debates over diverging views.

ONE	Write an introduction in which you present dialectical thinking as the skill of the future.
TWO	Write a paragraph in which you discuss *dialectical thinking for moral character*. Give examples, explanations, and details.
THREE	Write a paragraph in which you discuss *dialectical thinking at school, at work and other fields of life*. Give examples, explanations, and details.
FOUR	Write a paragraph in which you discuss *different ways to develop dialectical thinking*. Give examples, explanations, and details.
FIVE	Write a conclusion in which you discuss how important dialectical thinking is for an intelligent life.

CHAPTER 5

SKILLS IN LITERATURE AND FILMS

This chapter is meant to offer a different context to skills, that of fiction. Its activities are based on three short stories and three poems (which you can find online), and two films. You may read/watch all of them or one or two.

1. **DISCUSS THE SHORT STORY "NEW DIRECTIONS" BY MAYA ANGELOU**

    a. **In groups, discuss the questions below. Explain your views and offer examples.**

    1. Who is Annie Johnson?
    2. What is a disastrous marriage?
    3. Why is it burdensome that Annie Johnson is black?
    4. Does she know how she feels about her life?
    5. Does she do something about her dissatisfaction?
    6. Is Annie hesitant or in doubt before making a decision?
    7. Why does she decide to make a change without telling anyone?
    8. What kinds of skills does Annie possess?
    9. Does she know what she is good at?
    10. Does she know how to use her skills to her advantage?

    b. **Write a paragraph in which you summarize your discussion.**

2. **DISCUSS THE POEM "STILL I RISE" BY MAYA ANGELOU**

    a. **In groups, discuss the questions below. Explain your views and offer examples.**

    1. Who is the person speaking in the poem?
    2. What does she rise from?
    3. Who do you think she addresses in the poem?
    4. Who writes history and why would they lie?
    5. What are the skills of hope?
    6. What are the skills of the sun and the moon?
    7. What are the skills of the ocean?
    8. How can we shoot people with our words?
    9. How can we cut others with our eyes?
    10. What are the skills a person needs to rise from humiliations and pain?

b. Write a paragraph in which you summarize your discussion.

3. DISCUSS THE FILM "IRON JAWED ANGELS"

a. In groups, discuss the questions below. Explain your views and offer examples.

1. Who are the main characters in the film?
2. What are they fighting for and why?
3. Why don't men stand by their side?
4. How did they protest?
5. How did the government act to suppress their protests?
6. Is Alice Paul an example of courage? Explain.
7. What other skills do women in the film exhibit?
8. Is freedom of choice possible without freedom of speech?
9. Is physical pain a worse punishment than privation of freedom?
10. What are the skills a person needs to face resistance?

b. Write a paragraph in which you summarize your discussion.

4. DISCUSS CHANGE

a. In groups, discuss the questions below. Explain your views and offer examples.

1. What is the relation between change and age?
2. What makes change scary?
3. What makes change necessary?
4. Is change related in any way to self-knowledge?
5. What are the skills necessary to make change happen?

b. Write a paragraph in which you summarize your discussion.

5. DISCUSS COURAGE

a. In groups, discuss the questions below. Explain your views and offer examples.

1. What are the hardships people usually face in life?
2. Are people just born with courage or do they develop it?
3. Is it possible to deal with difficulties without courage?
4. What are the skills necessary to develop courage?
5. Comment on the following statement: *You develop courage by dealing with rejections as inevitable parts of life. But most of all, you develop courage by seeing yourself free.*

b. Write a paragraph in which you summarize your discussion.

6. DISCUSS CONFIDENCE

a. In groups, discuss the questions below. Explain your views and offer examples.

1. What makes a person seem confident?
2. What makes a person feel confident?
3. Are we born confident or do we develop this skill?
4. Is happiness possible without confidence?
5. What other personal skills are related to confidence?

b. Write a paragraph in which you summarize your discussion.

7. DISCUSS PERSEVERANCE

a. In groups, discuss the questions below. Explain your views and offer examples.

1. When do we people feel broken?
2. Is it easy to act when you feel broken?

3. Can you still feel proud when others degrade you?
4. What makes a person persevere when everything seems hard?
5. What other skills are related to perseverance?

b. **Write a paragraph in which you summarize your discussion.**

8. WRITE AN ESSAY

Use all your previous notes and write an essay in which you discuss the statement below. Use evidence from the short story "New Directions", the poem "Still I Rise" and the film "Iron Jawed Angels". You can follow the guiding instructions provided below. Remember to give your essay a title.

It is never too late to change directions in life, but it takes a lot of courage and perseverance to do so.

ONE	Write an introduction in which you point out the importance of change in certain situations of life. Also, mention some important skills necessary to make change happen.
TWO	Write a paragraph in which you discuss *courage* as a necessary skill to cause change. Give examples, explanations, and details.
THREE	Write a paragraph in which you discuss *perseverance* as an essential skill to make change happen. Give examples, explanations, and details.
FOUR	Write a paragraph in which you discuss other important *skills* (such as patience, diligence, meticulousness) necessary to make your dreams come true. Give examples, explanations, and details.
FIVE	Write a conclusion in which you discuss how important courage, perseverance, and other skills are to make one's life better.

9. DISCUSS THE POEM "IF" BY RUDYARD KIPLING

a. In groups, discuss the questions below. Explain your views and offer examples.

1. Who is the poet addressing in the poem?
2. What does it take to keep one's head when others lose theirs?
3. What does it take to trust yourself when others doubt you?
4. When are dreams masters over the dreamer?
5. What are the implications of making thoughts your aims?
6. What skills does one need to rebuild one's broken life?
7. What skills does one need to risk all winnings?
8. What skills does one need to never say a word about one's loss?
9. How can you be virtuous when you have power and by fame?
10. What are the skills a person needs to be immune to hurt?

b. Write a paragraph in which you summarize your discussion.

10. DISCUSS THE POEM "DESIDERATA" BY MAX EHRMANN

a. In groups, discuss the questions below. Explain your views and offer examples.

1. Who is the poet addressing in the poem?
2. How does the poet advise us to speak and listen to others?
3. What happens to us when we always compare ourselves with others?
4. Is it easy to enjoy one's achievements while making plans for the future?
5. Why is it important to keep interested in one's career?
6. Do you agree that the career is a real possession in a world of change?
7. Are all people in one way or another the heroes of their lives?
8. How can you be yourself when different situations need you to adapt and conform?
9. What does the passage of years teach us about aspirations and dreams?
10. What are the skills a person needs to develop in a world of deception and broken dreams?

b. **Write a paragraph in which you summarize your discussion.**

11. DISCUSS EQUANIMITY

a. **In groups, discuss the questions below. Explain your views and offer examples.**

1. What makes a person seem calm?
2. What makes a person feel calm?
3. Are we born self-possessed or do we develop this skill?
4. Is happiness possible without equanimity?
5. What other personal skills are related to self-possession?

b. **Write a paragraph in which you summarize your discussion.**

12. DISCUSS HUMILITY

a. **In groups, discuss the questions below. Explain your views and offer examples.**

1. When do people achieve power and fame?
2. Is it easy to be humble when one is powerful?
3. When do people have strong beliefs and convictions?
4. How can a person accept others' opinions when they are convinced of theirs?
5. What other skills are related to humility?

b. **Write a paragraph in which you summarize your discussion.**

13. DISCUSS DISCIPLINE

a. In groups, discuss the questions below. Explain your views and offer examples.

1. What is a disciplined mind?
2. How is discipline connected to the unpredictability of life?
3. How can we discipline the mind to deal with emotions?
4. How can we discipline the mind to stop comparing us with other people?
5. What other skills are necessary to develop a disciplined mind?

b. Write a paragraph in which you summarize your discussion.

14. DISCUSS TRANQUILITY

a. In groups, discuss the questions below. Explain your views and offer examples.

1. How can one go tranquilly when others go in hurriedness?
2. Is it easy to be content when the world encourages you to aspire for more?
3. When do people become bitter and self-absorbed?
4. How can one be always honest and agreeable at the same time?
5. What other skills are related to tranquility?

b. Write a paragraph in which you summarize your discussion.

15. WRITE AN ESSAY

Use all your previous notes and write an essay in which you discuss the statement below. Use evidence from the poems "If" by Rudyard Kipling and "Desiderata" by Max Ehrmann. You can follow the guiding instructions provided below. Remember to give your essay a title.

A meaningful life entails enjoying control over oneself rather than control over others.

ONE	Write an introduction in which you point out the importance of self-control for a peaceful life. Also, mention some important skills necessary to enjoy such a frame of mind.
TWO	Write a paragraph in which you discuss *equanimity* as a necessary skill to master in a world of noise and haste. Give examples, explanations, and details.
THREE	Write a paragraph in which you discuss *humility* as an essential skill to live a life of self-determination. Give examples, explanations, and details.
FOUR	Write a paragraph in which you discuss other important *skills* (such as discipline and active listening) necessary to make life manageable. Give examples, explanations, and details.
FIVE	Write a conclusion in which you discuss how significant equanimity, humility, and other skills are to make one's life meaningful.

16. DISCUSS THE STORY "A PAIR OF SILK STOCKINGS" BY KATE CHOPIN

a. In groups, discuss the questions below. Explain your views and offer examples.

1. Who is Missus Sommers?
2. Why is it difficult for her to decide what to spend the money on?
3. What do we learn about her present life?
4. What do we learn about her past life?
5. Is she happy with her present life?
6. Is she a spontaneous or a calculated person?
7. Is spontaneity a great skill?
8. Is she a responsible parent?
9. Is she a self-sacrificing mother?
10. What are her greatest skills?

b. **Write a paragraph in which you summarize your discussion.**

17. DISCUSS THE STORY "THE GIFT OF THE MAGI" BY O. HENRY

a. **In groups, discuss the questions below. Explain your views and offer examples.**

1. Who are Della and Jim?
2. What do we learn about their life?
3. Are they happy together?
4. Are they devoted to each other?
5. Would Christmas be the same without gifts?
6. What kinds of feelings make a person give up what they treasure the most?
7. Would life without gifts be more or less exciting?
8. Is money an important element in the happiness of a couple?
9. Does love demand that we give more or that we receive more?
10. What are the skills necessary for a successful relationship?

b. **Write a paragraph in which you summarize your discussion.**

18. DISCUSS THE FILM "OF MICE AND MEN"

a. **In groups, discuss the questions below. Explain your views and offer examples.**

1. Who are the characters in the film?
2. Why do they move from place to place?
3. What is their dream?
4. What are the obstacles that stand in their way?
5. What makes loneliness an important theme?
6. What makes George determined to take care of Lennie?
7. What can we guess about George's feelings from his actions?

8. How do we know that Lennie feels powerless?
9. Is it wrong or admirable that George sacrifices himself for Lennie?
10. What are the skills necessary to dedicate your life to others?

b. **Write a paragraph in which you summarize your discussion.**

19. DISCUSS INDULGENCE

a. **In groups, discuss the questions below. Explain your views and offer examples.**

1. What is indulgence and when do we indulge?
2. Does indulgence always entail lack of willpower?
3. Do we indulge because we are happy or because we are unhappy?
4. Should everybody indulge sometimes?
5. Are you morally superior if you never indulge?

b. **Write a paragraph in which you summarize your discussion.**

20. DISCUSS RESPONSIBILITY

a. **In groups, discuss the questions below. Explain your views and offer examples.**

1. Is being a parent giving up personal desires?
2. Is parental responsibility always related to self-renunciation?
3. Is being responsible the same as being in control?
4. Is being in control the same as dependable?
5. What other skills are related to responsibility?

b. **Write a paragraph in which you summarize your discussion.**

21. DISCUSS SELF-SACRIFICE

a. In groups, discuss the questions below. Explain your views and offer examples.

1. Is self-sacrifice possible without love?
2. Is self-sacrifice compatible with self-respect?
3. Is a self-sacrificing parent different from a self-sacrificing lover?
4. Can self-sacrifice be excluded from a successful relationship?
5. What are some important skills connected to self-sacrifice?

b. Write a paragraph in which you summarize your discussion.

22. DISCUSS MOTIVATION

a. In groups, discuss the questions below. Explain your views and offer examples.

1. What are some of the feelings that motivate our behavior?
2. Does love motivate us in a different way than respect?
3. What motivates us in a relationship?
4. What motivates us in a job?
5. Which is the best motivating guide: emotions or reason?

b. Write a paragraph in which you summarize your discussion.

23. WRITE AN ESSAY

Use all your previous notes and write an essay in which you discuss the statement below. Use evidence from the short stories "A Pair of Silk Stockings" by Kate Chopin and "The Gift of the Magi" by O. Henry, as well as the film "Of Mice and Men". You can follow the guiding instructions provided below. Remember to give your essay a title.

Almost all relationships require self-sacrifice, but sometimes self-indulgence is the only way to live an authentic life.

ONE	Write an introduction in which you point out the importance of self-sacrifice and self-indulgence for a good life. Also, mention some important skills necessary to enjoy such a life.
TWO	Write a paragraph in which you discuss *self-sacrifice* as a necessary skill for a successful relationship. Give examples, explanations, and details.
THREE	Write a paragraph in which you discuss *self-indulgence* as necessary to live an authentic life. Give examples, explanations, and details.
FOUR	Write a paragraph in which you discuss other important *skills* (such as responsibility and motivation) necessary to make the right choices. Give examples, explanations, and details.
FIVE	Write a conclusion in which you discuss how significant self-sacrifice, self-indulgence, and other skills are to make one's life meaningful.

REFERENCES

Angelo, Maya. 1994. "New Direction" from *Wouldn't Take Nothing for My Journey Now*. Bantam Edition.
Angelo, Maya. 1994. "Still I Rise" from *The Complete Collected Poems of Maya Angelou*. Random House.
Chopin, Kate. 2006. "A Pair of Silk Stockings" from *The Complete Works of Kate Chopin*. Baton Rouge: Louisiana State University Press.
Ehrman, Max. 1927. "Desiderata" retrieved on 17.04.19 from https://allpoetry.com/Desiderata---Words-for-Life.
Eliot, T.S. 1941. "If" from *A Choice of Kipling's Verse*. London: Faber and Faber Ltd.
Henry. O. The gift of the Magi retrieved on 17.04.19 from http://www.eastoftheweb.com/short-stories/UBooks/GifMag.shtml.
Iron jawed Angels. 2004. Historical drama directed by Katja von Garnier.
Of Mice and Men.1992. Drama film directed by Gary Sinise.

www.ingramcontent.com/pod-product-compliance
Lightning Source LLC
Chambersburg PA
CBHW080612230426
43664CB00019B/2869